Tenderness

Bedded on decay

Rubs temperature

Into the light of colour

Until what envisions itself

Appears layering

And condensing

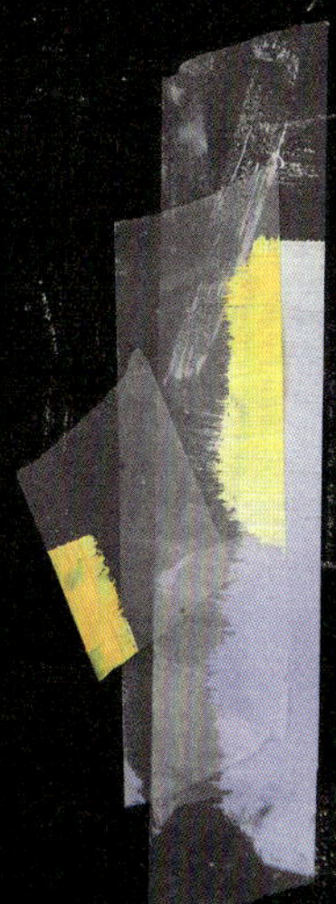

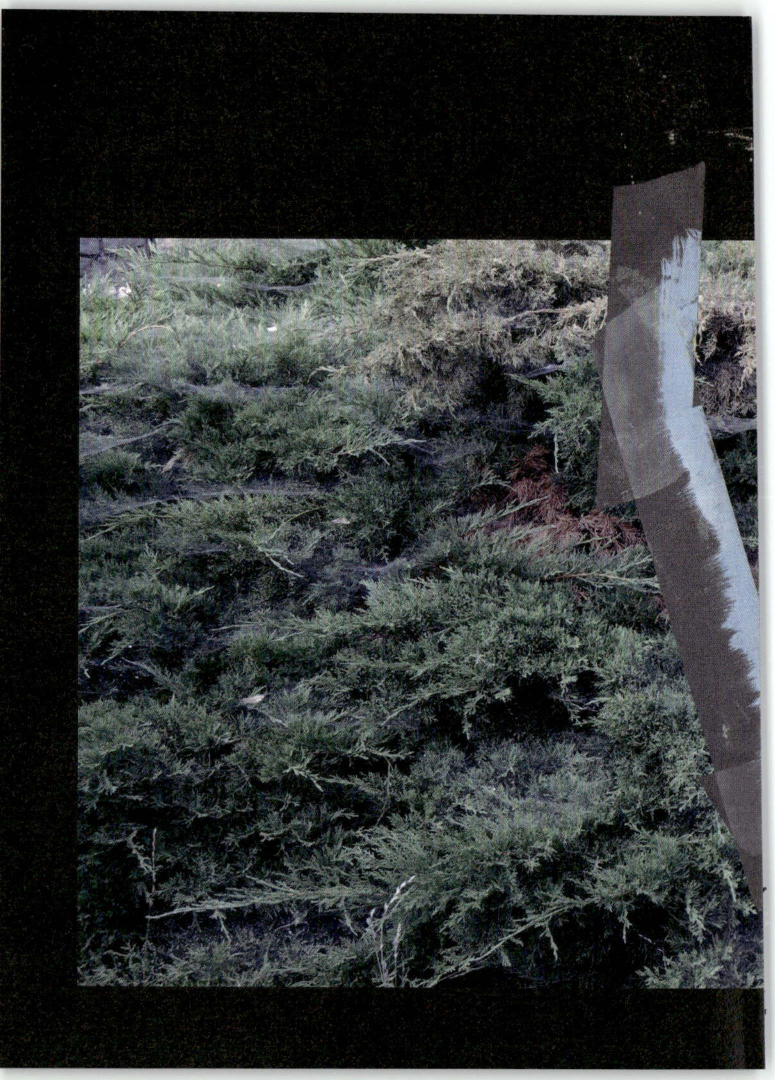

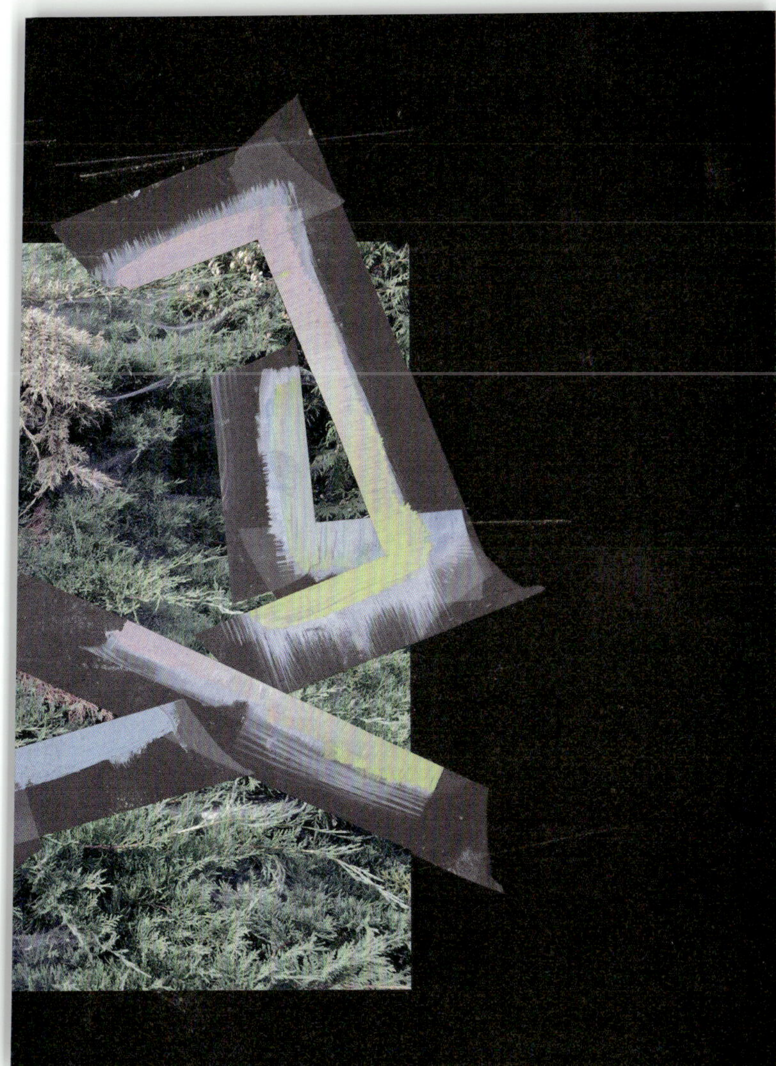

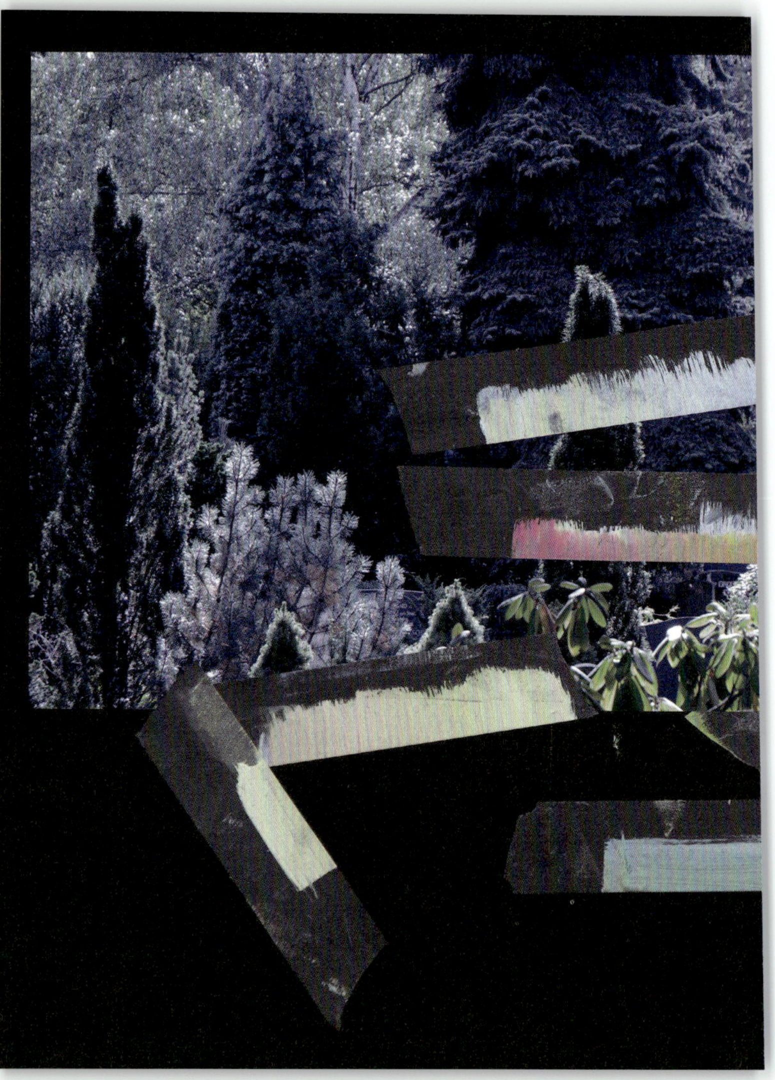

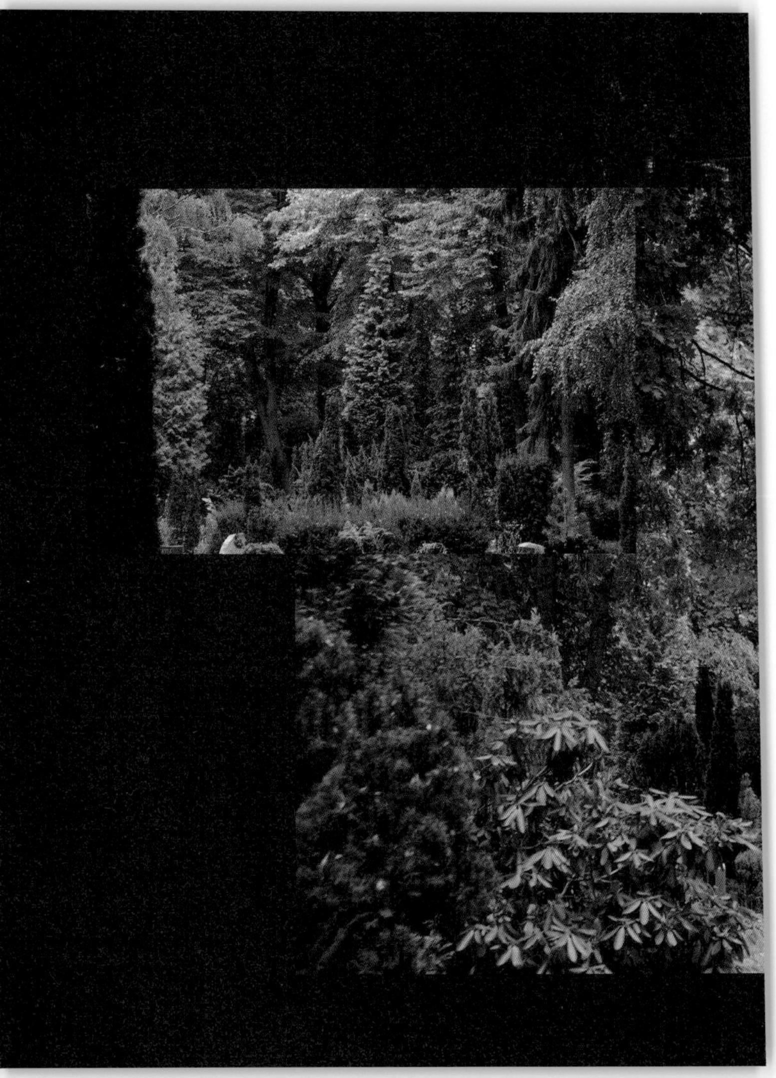

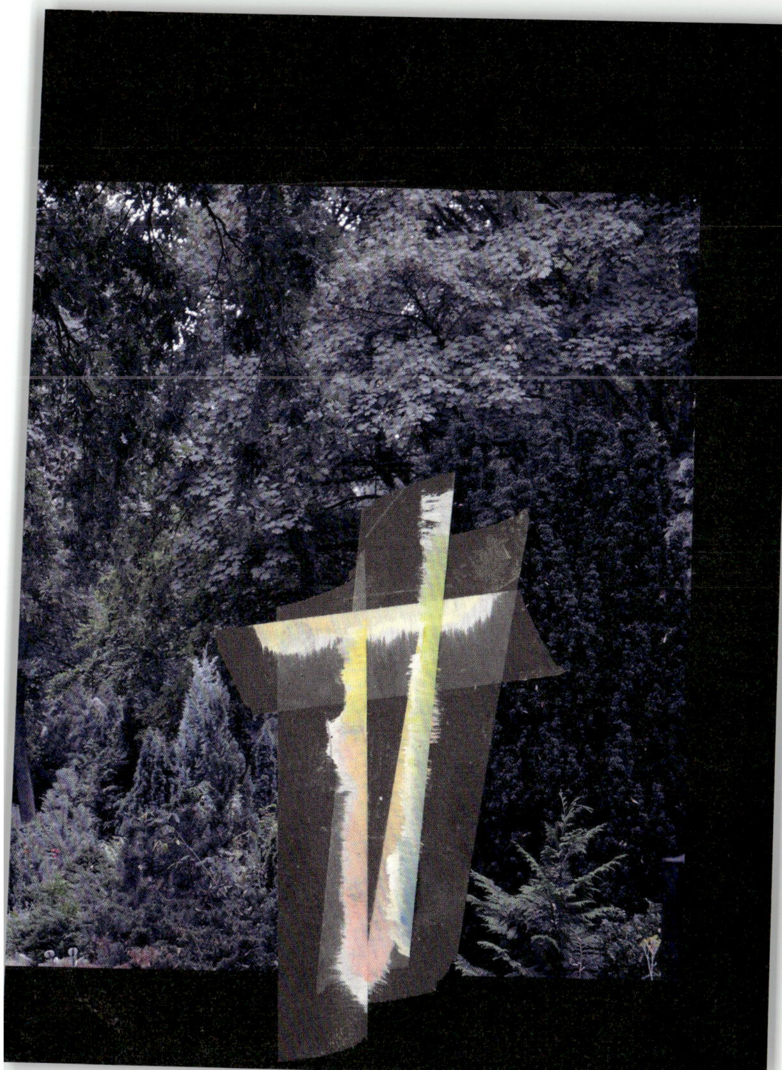

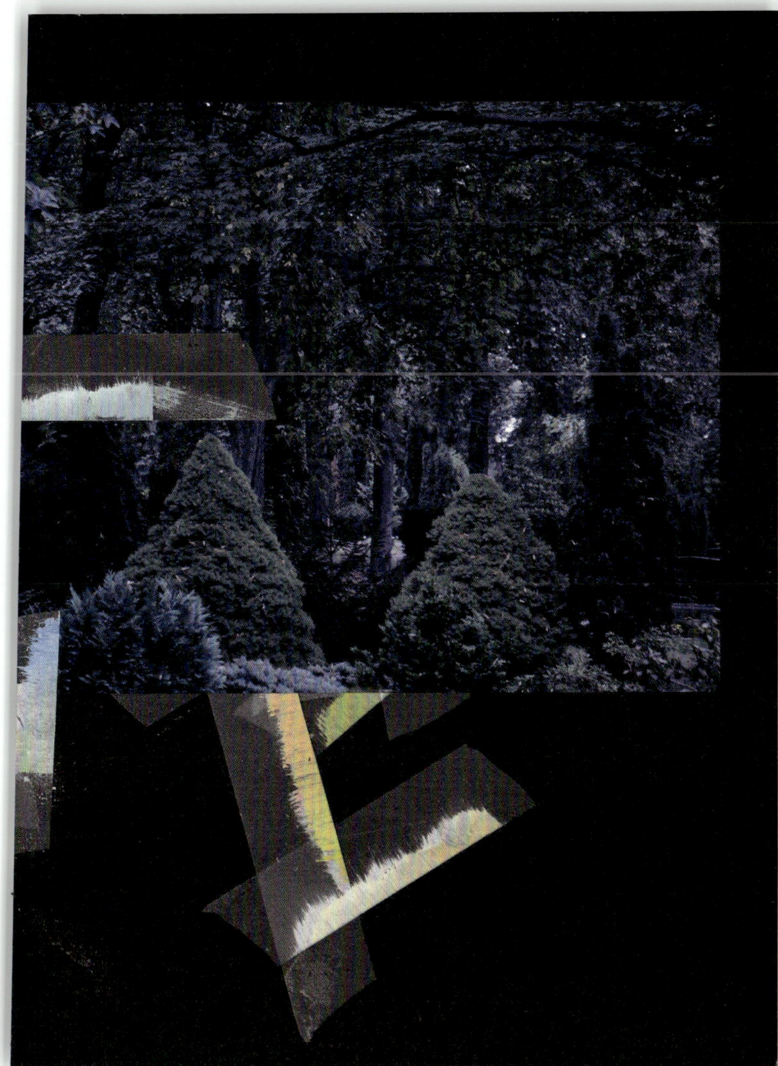

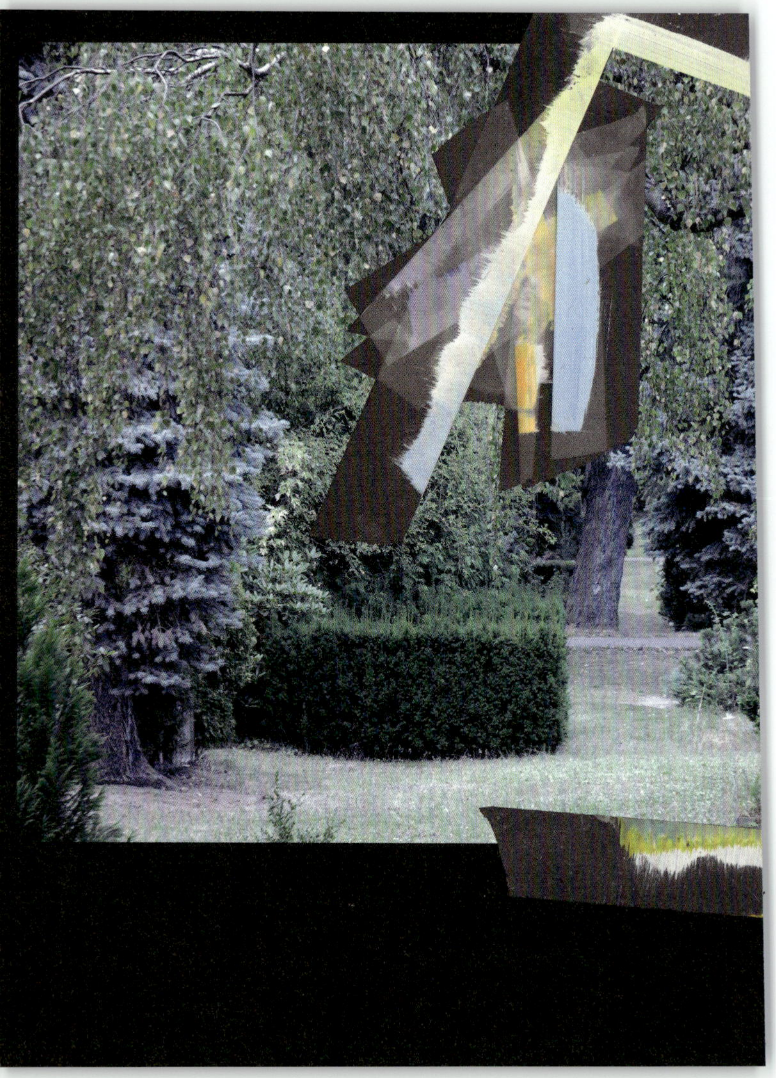

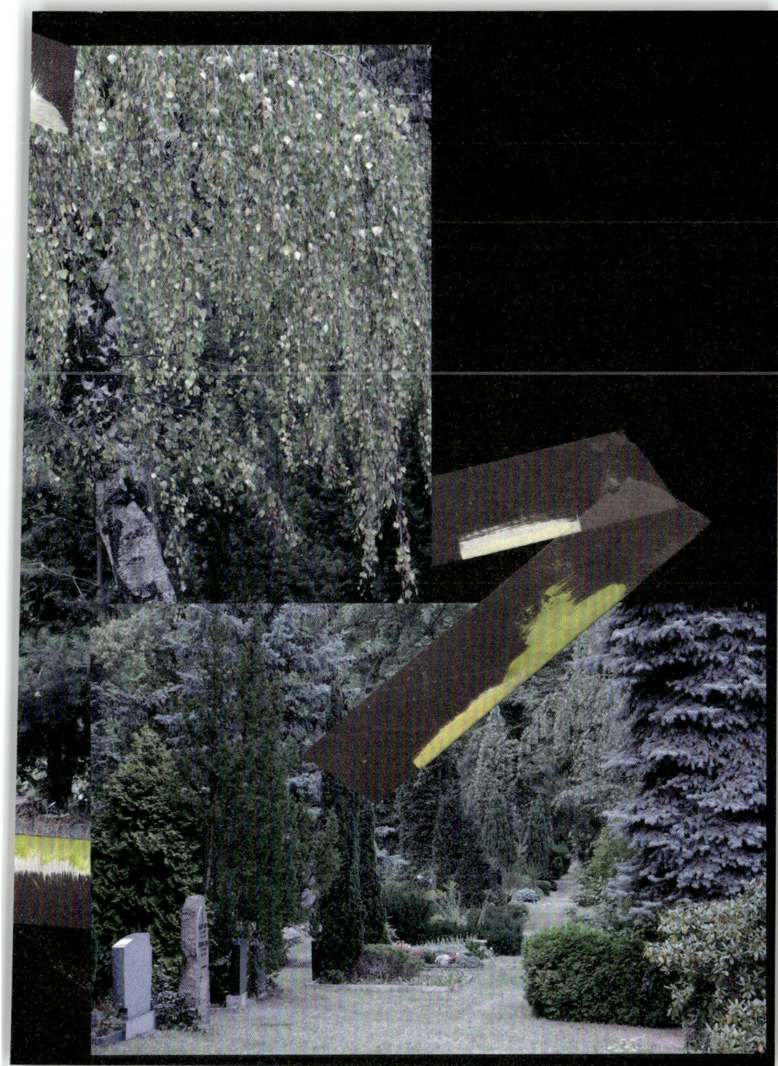

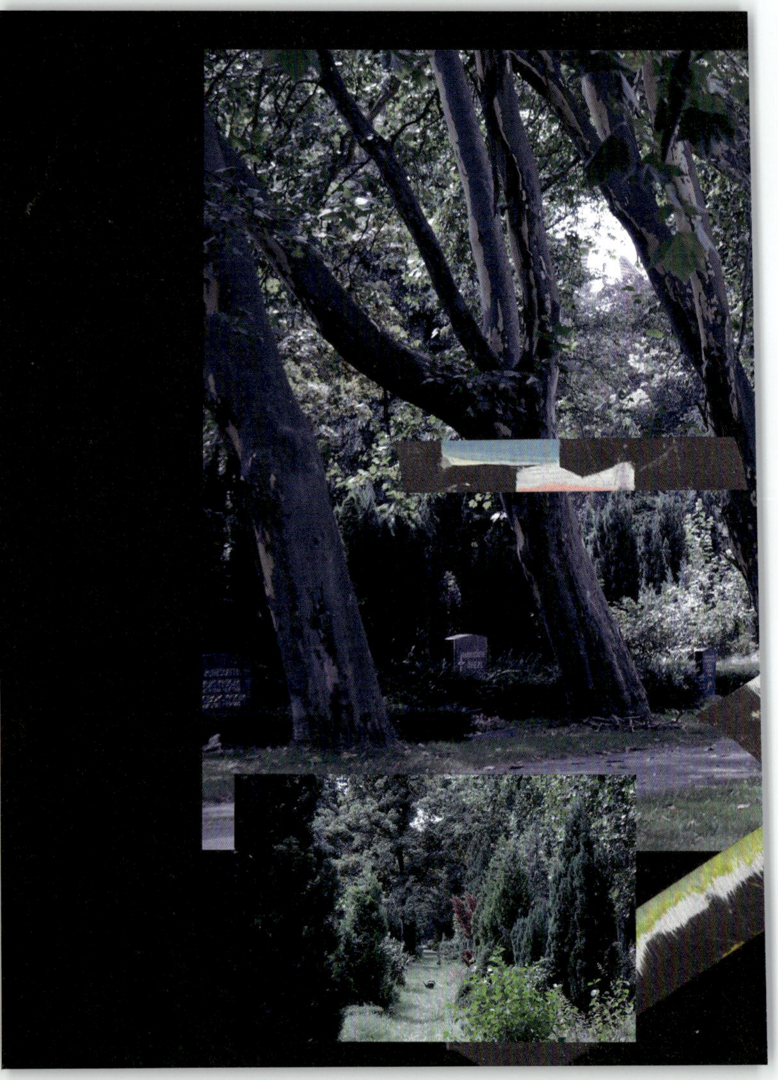

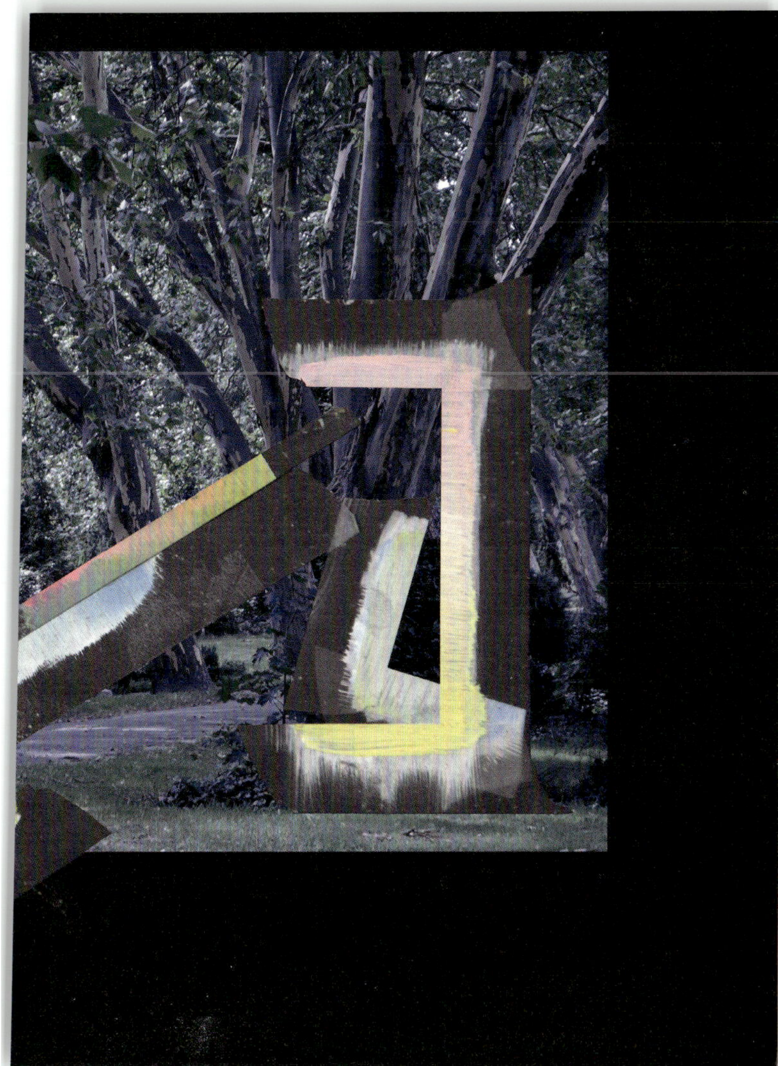

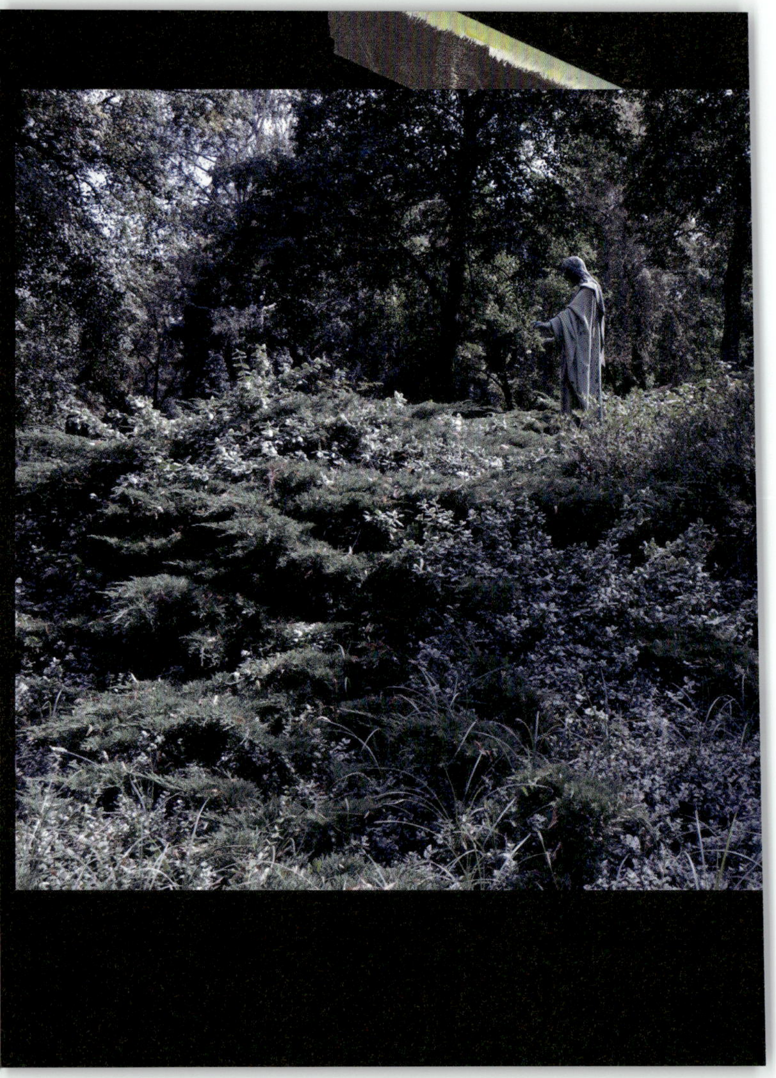

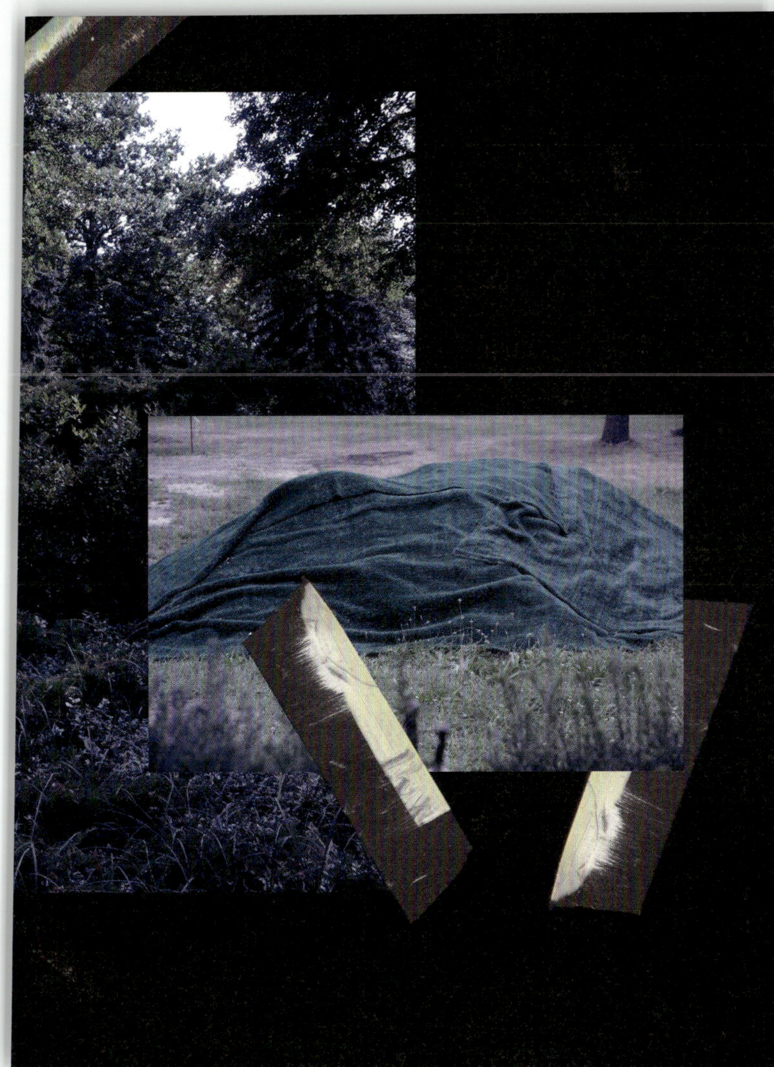

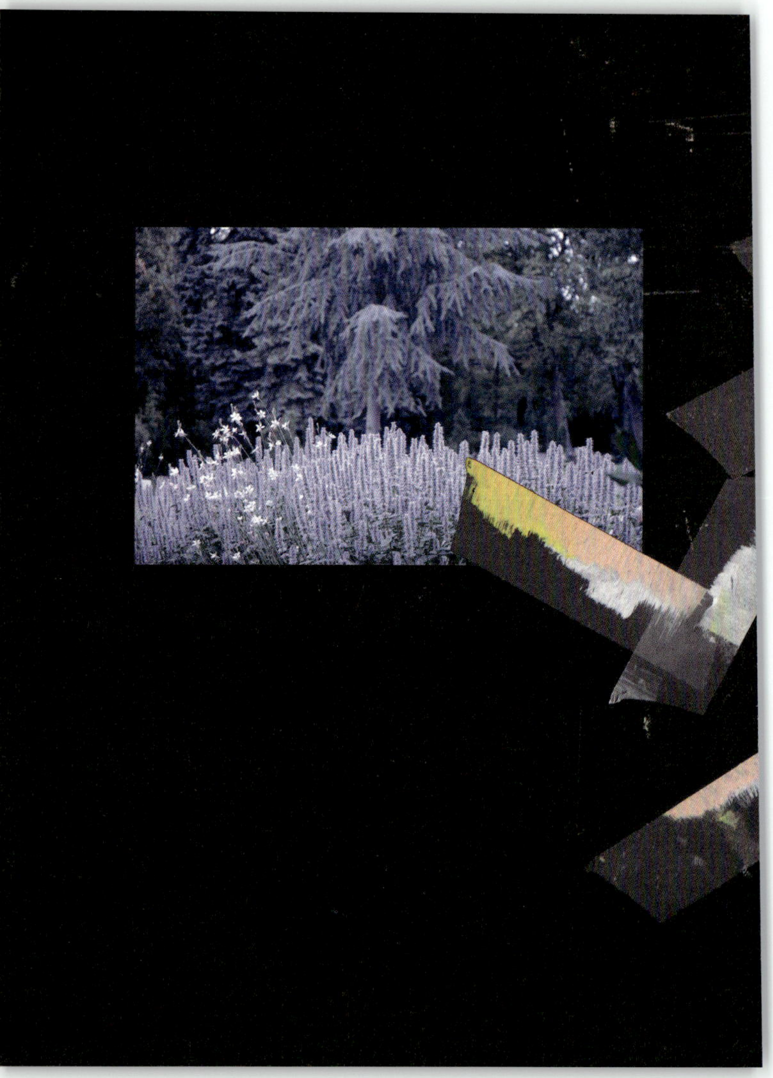

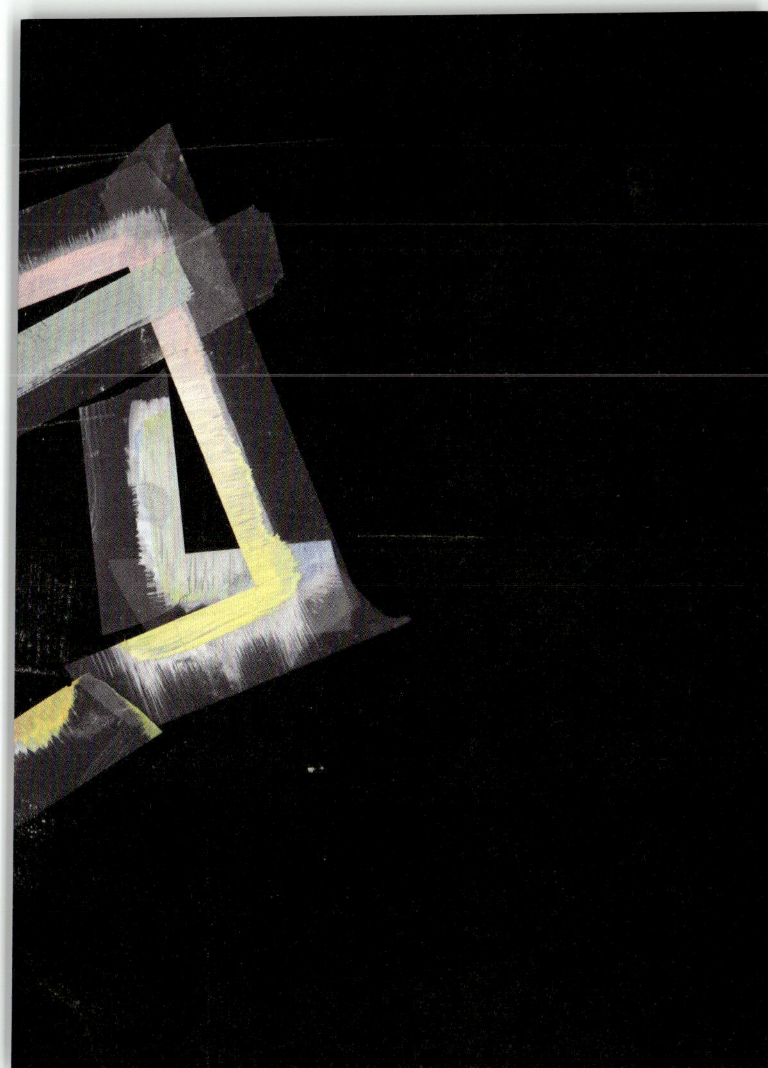

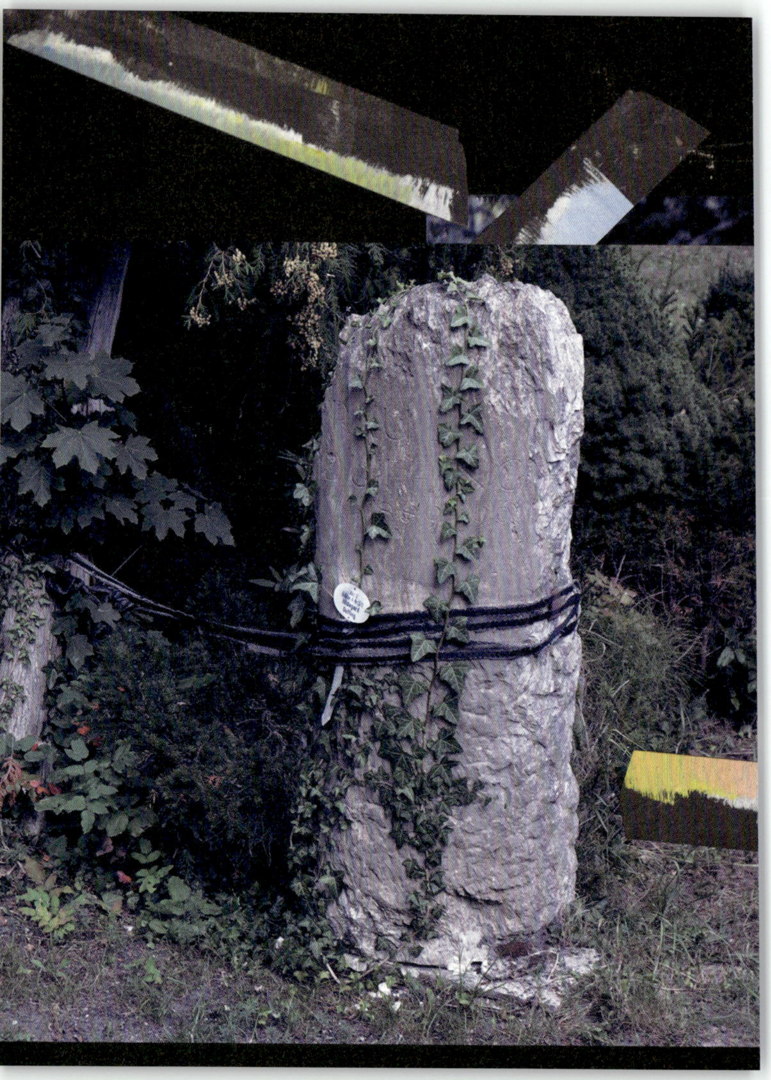

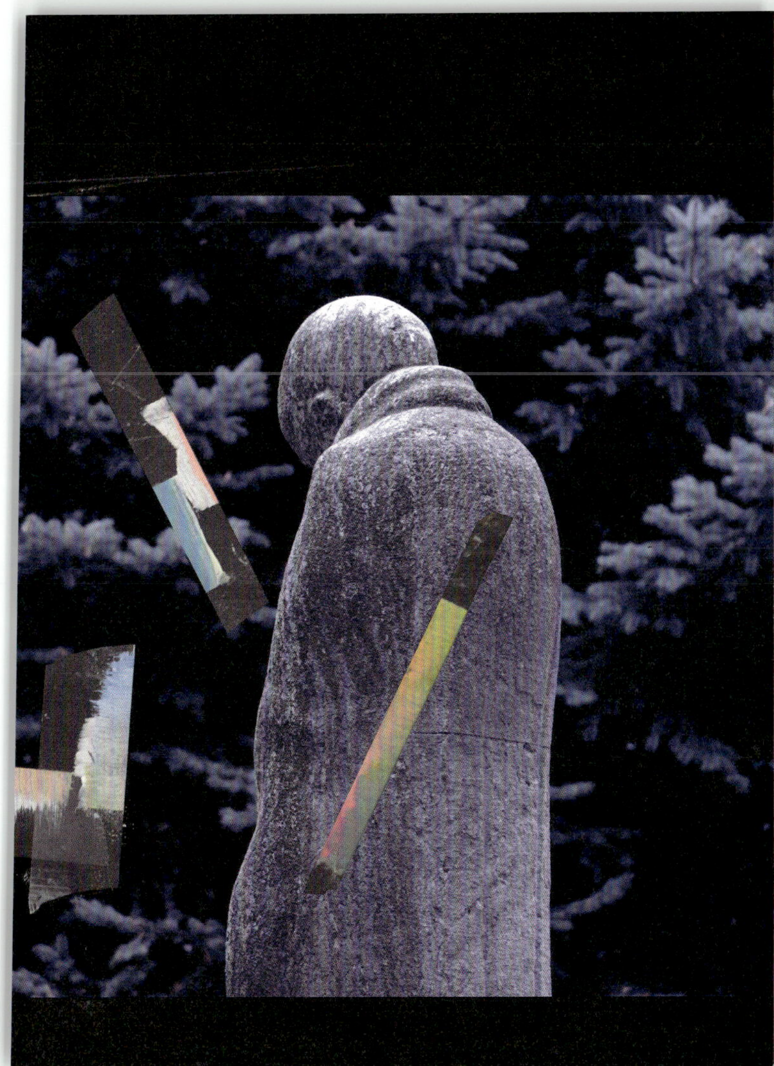

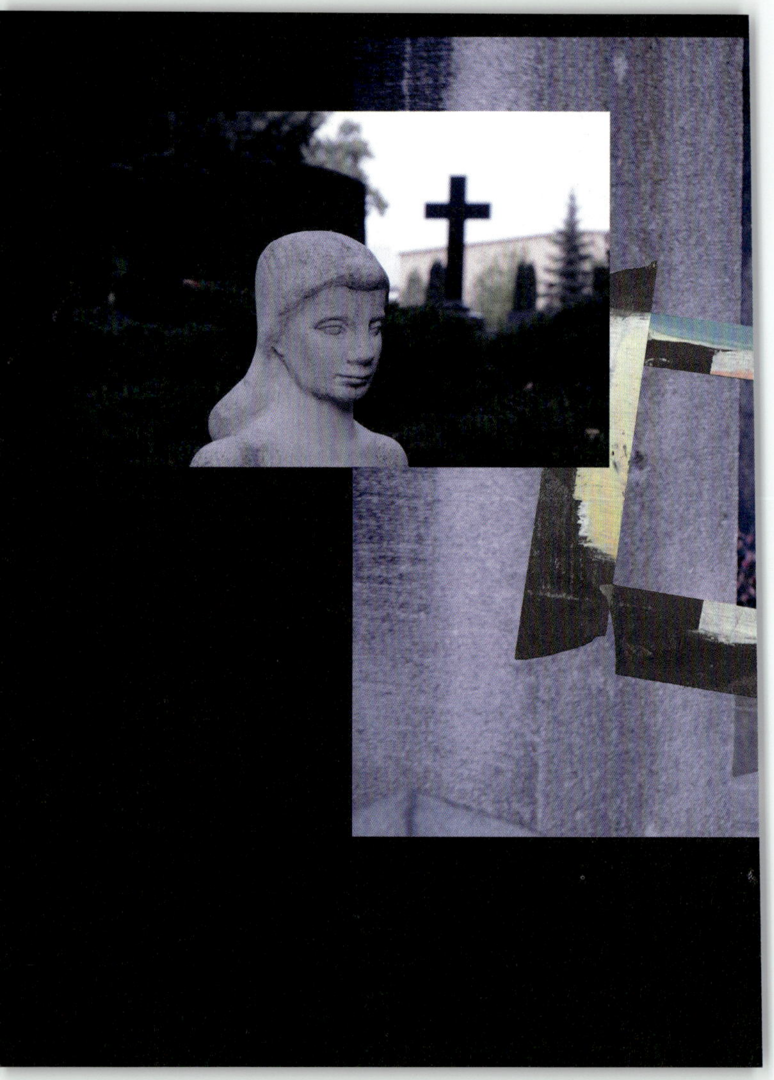

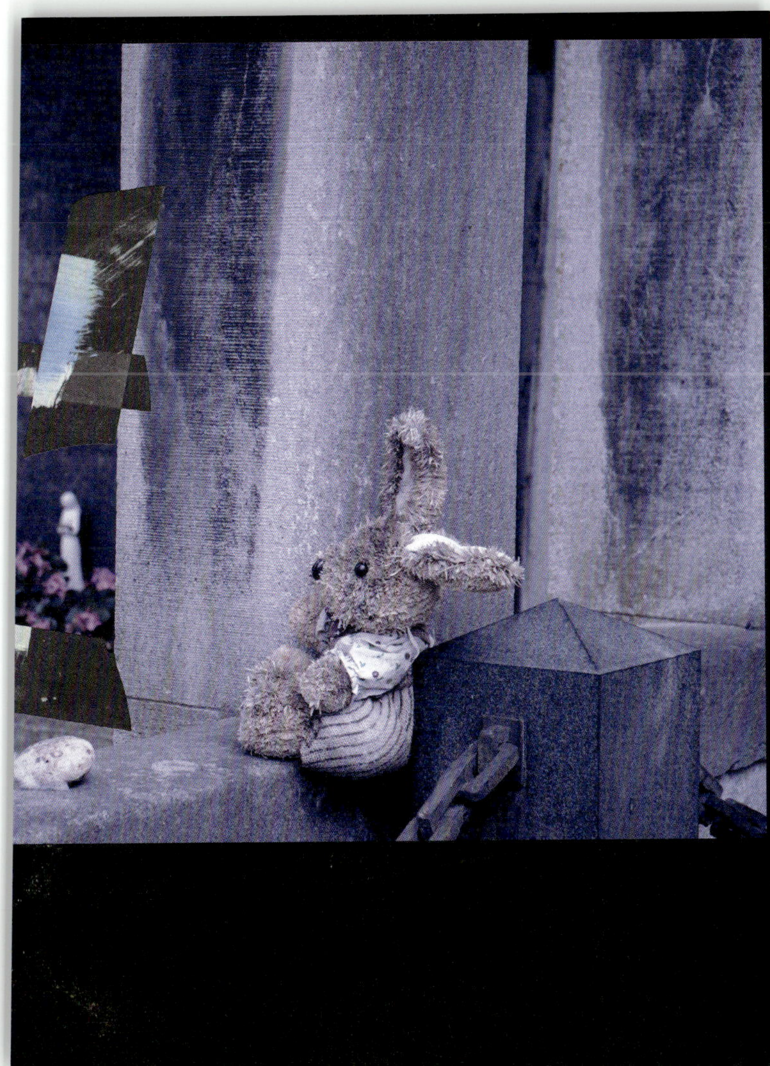

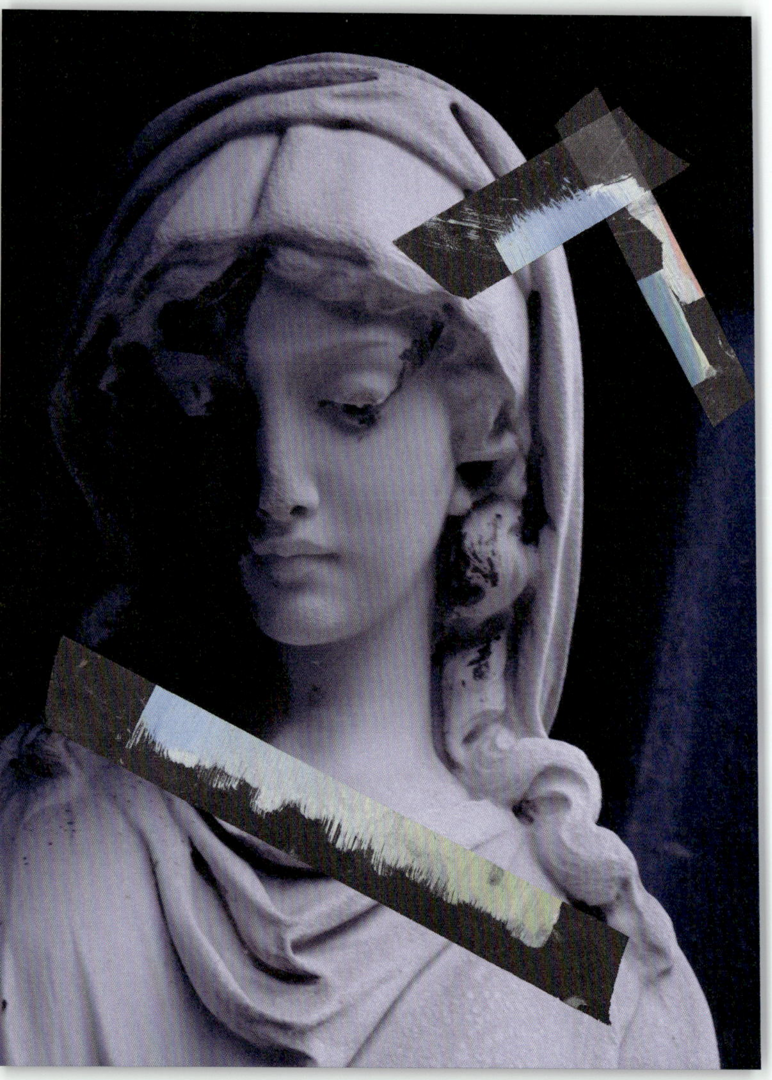

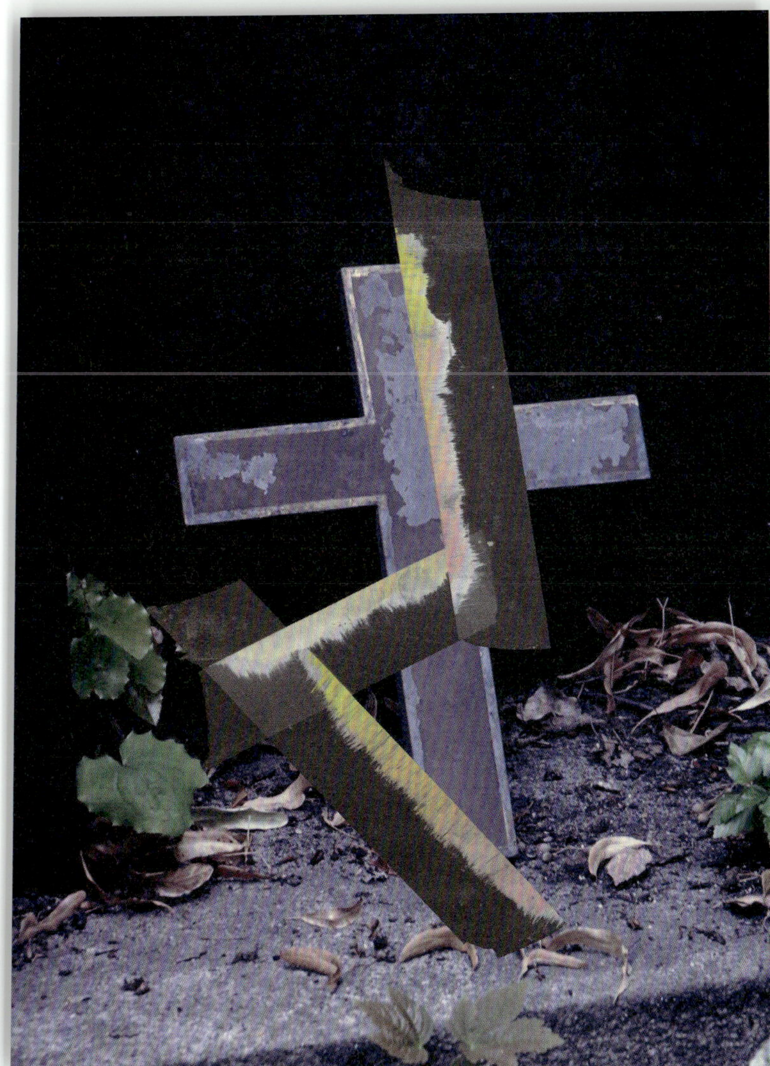

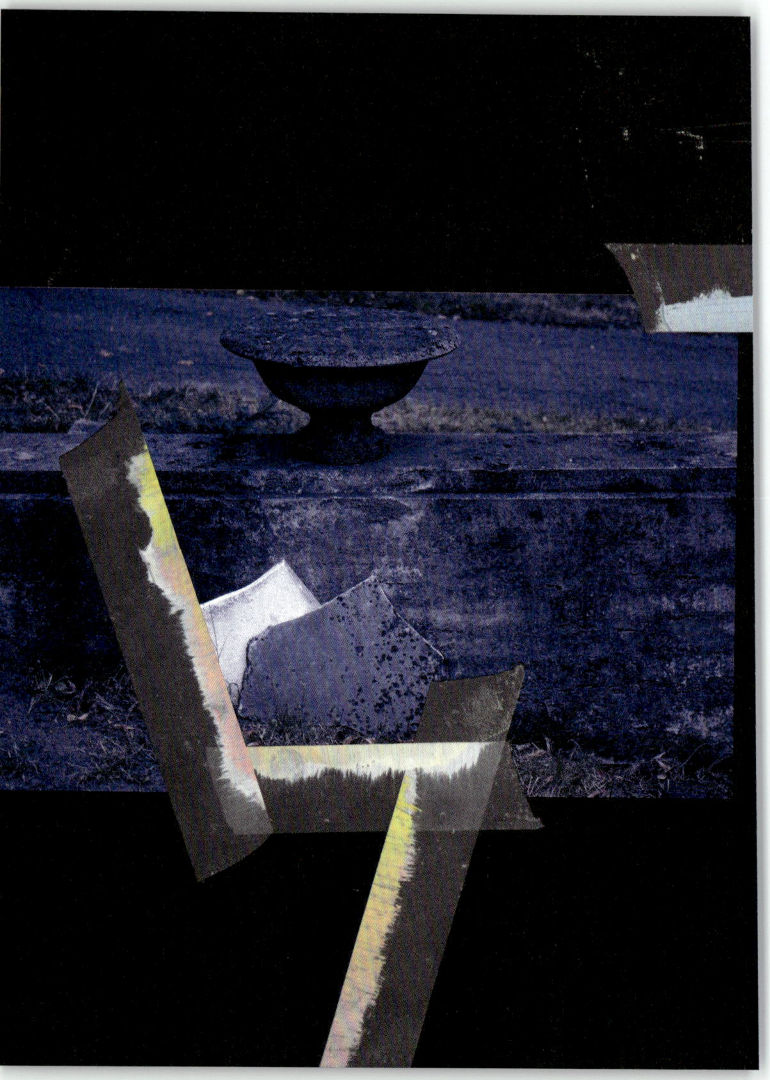

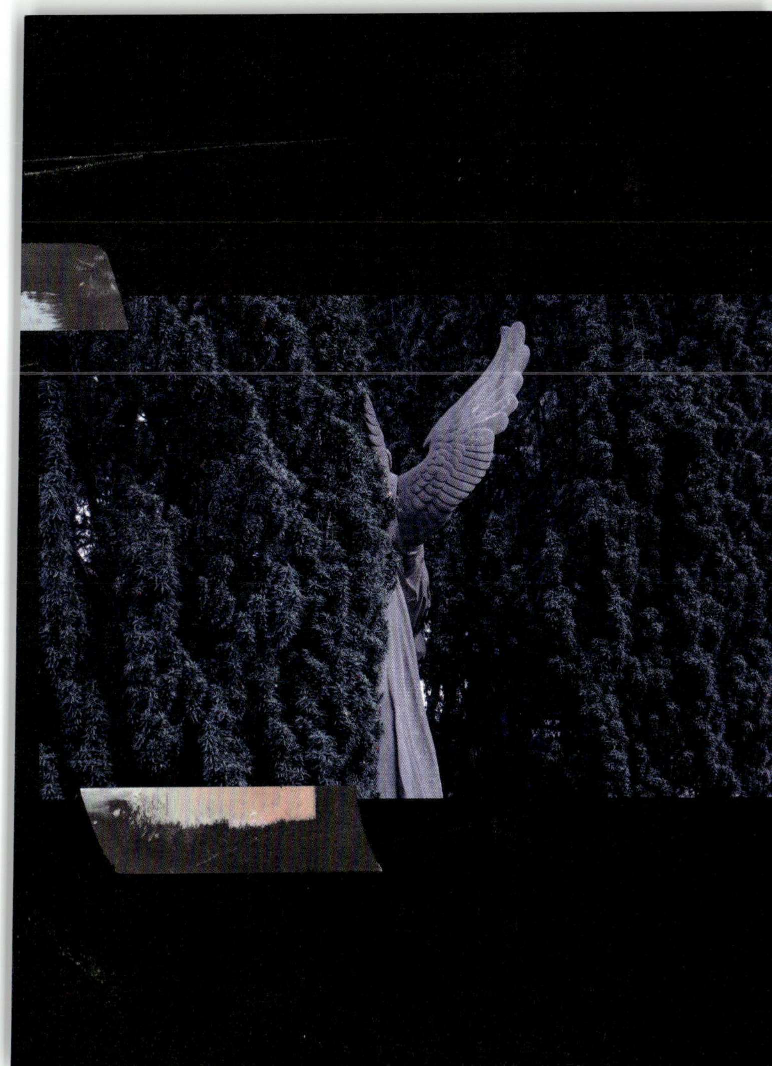

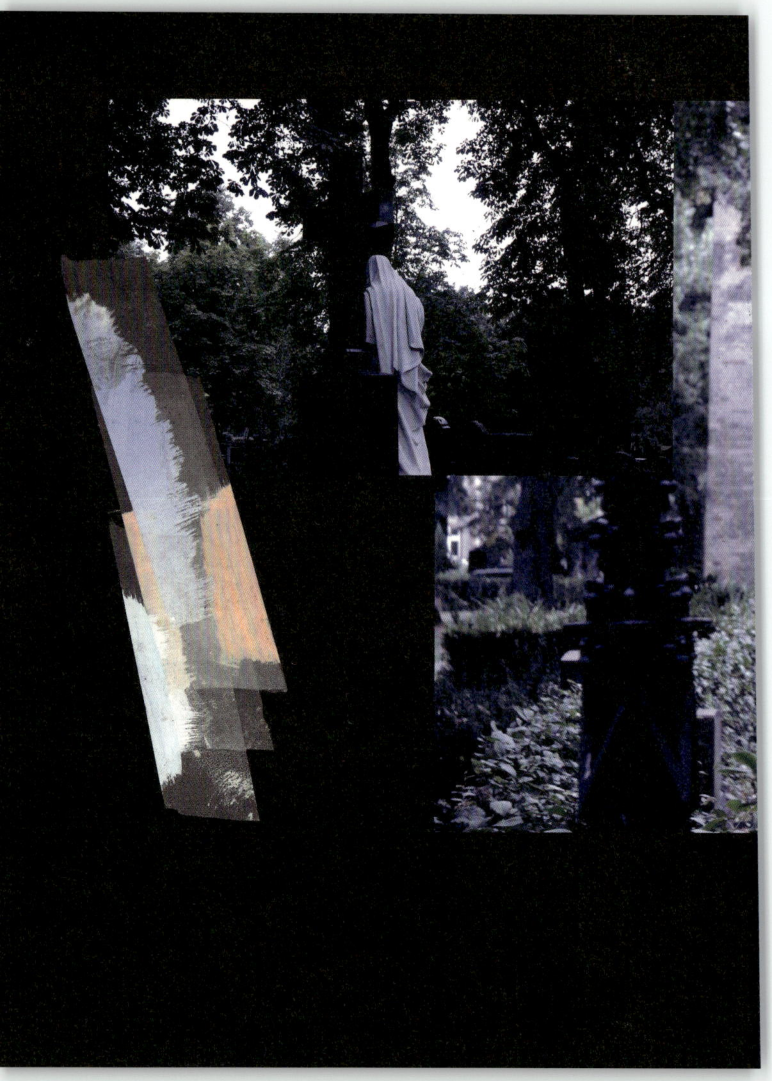

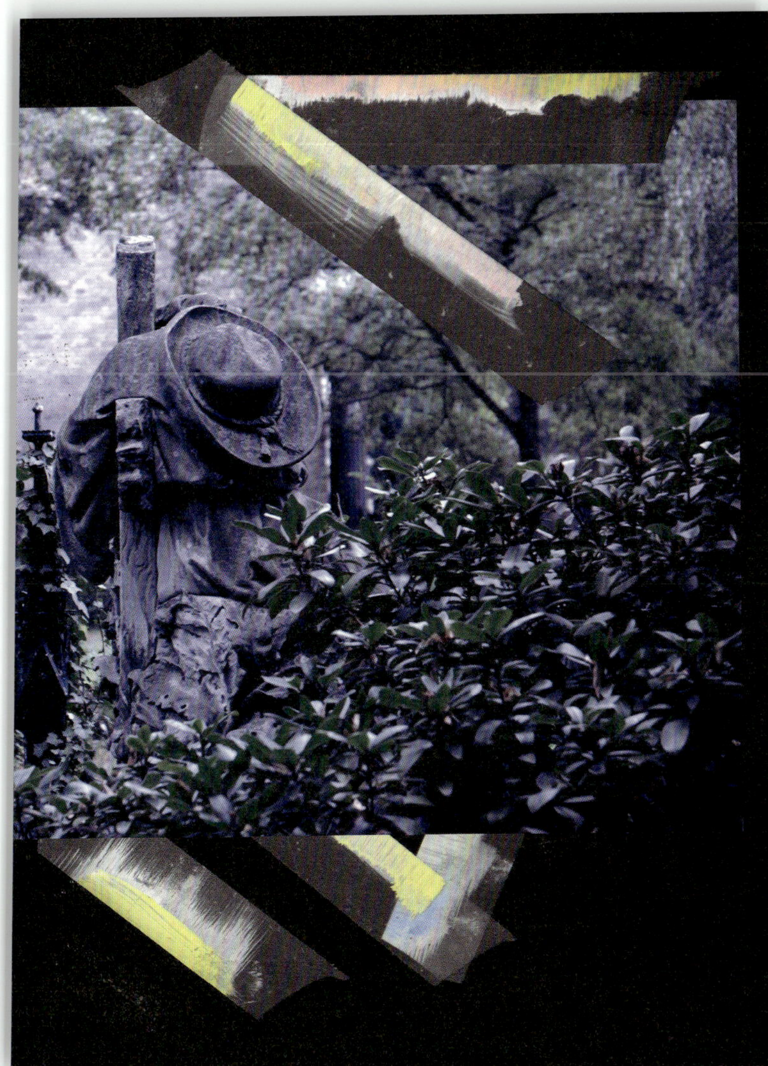

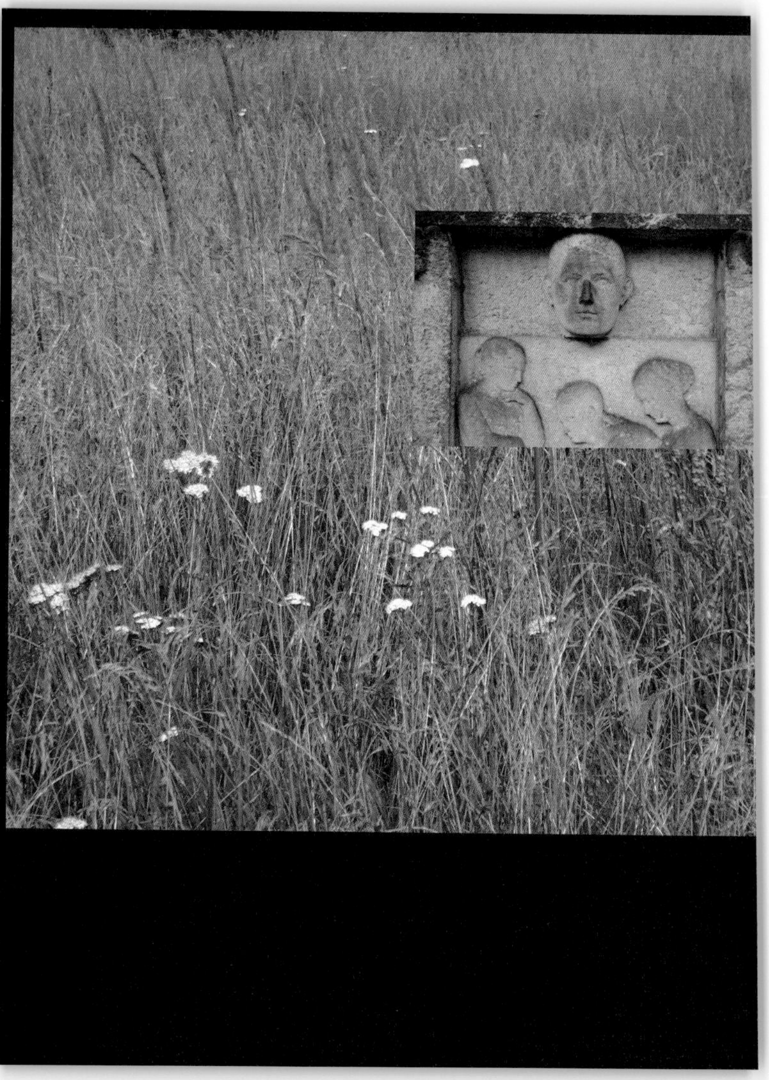

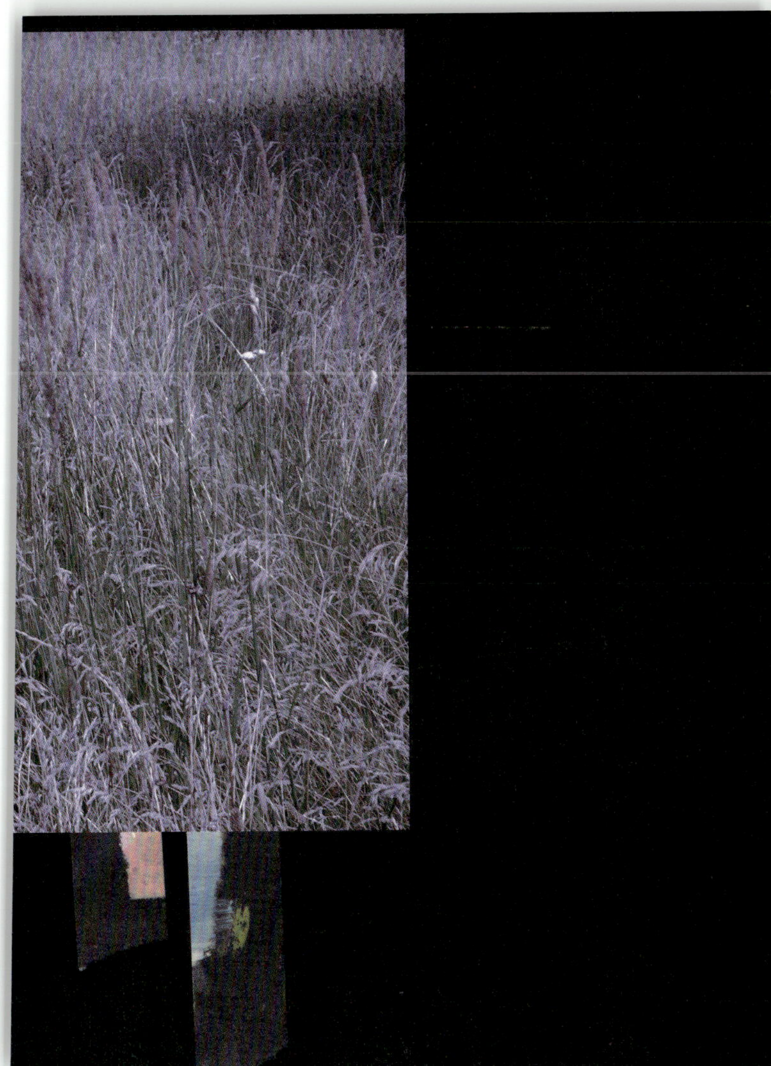

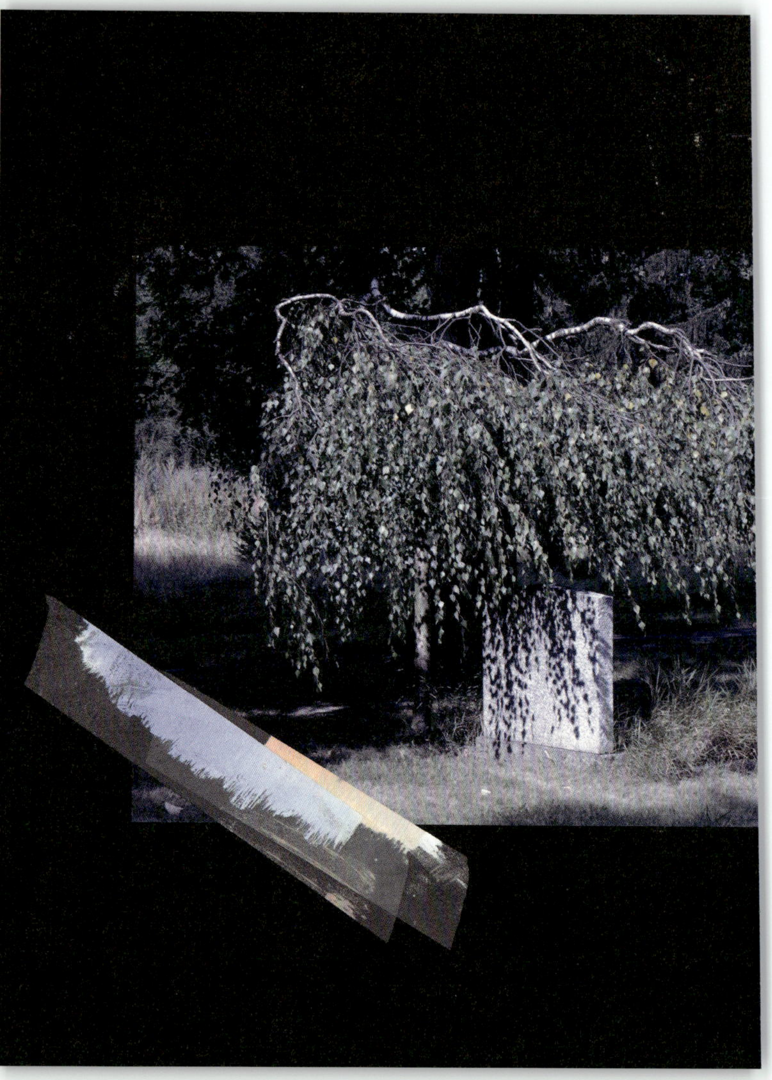

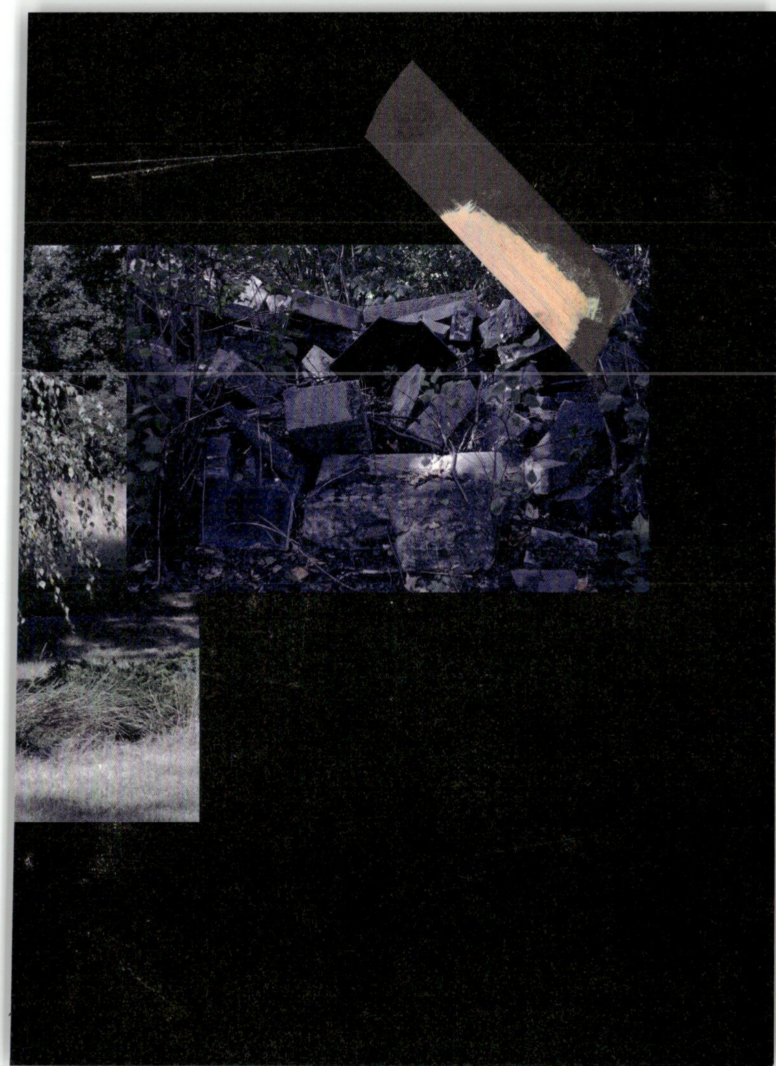

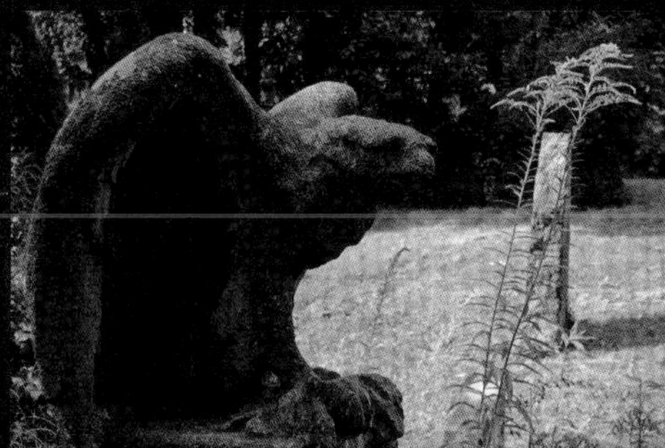

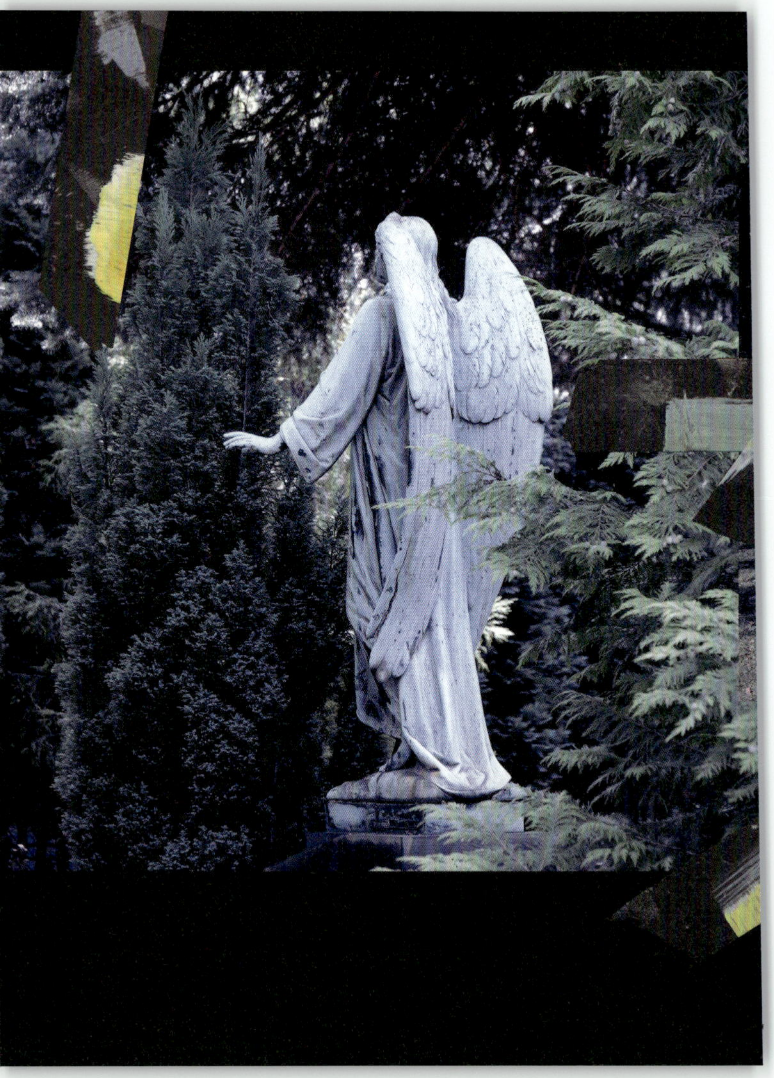

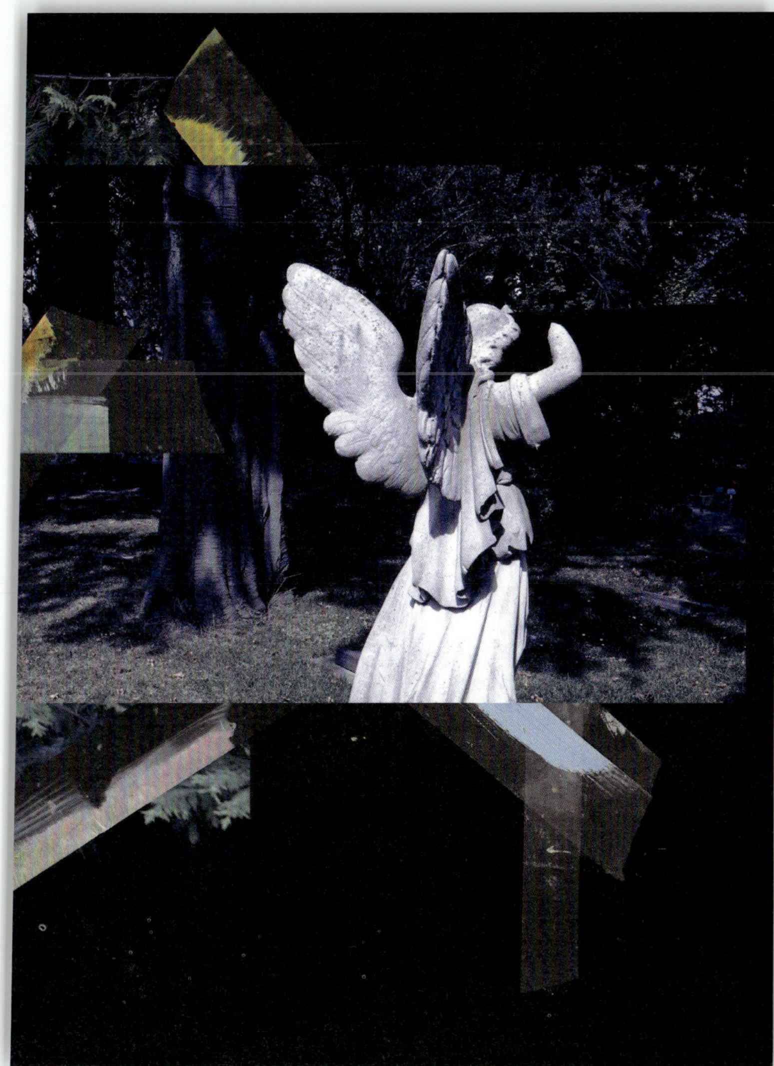

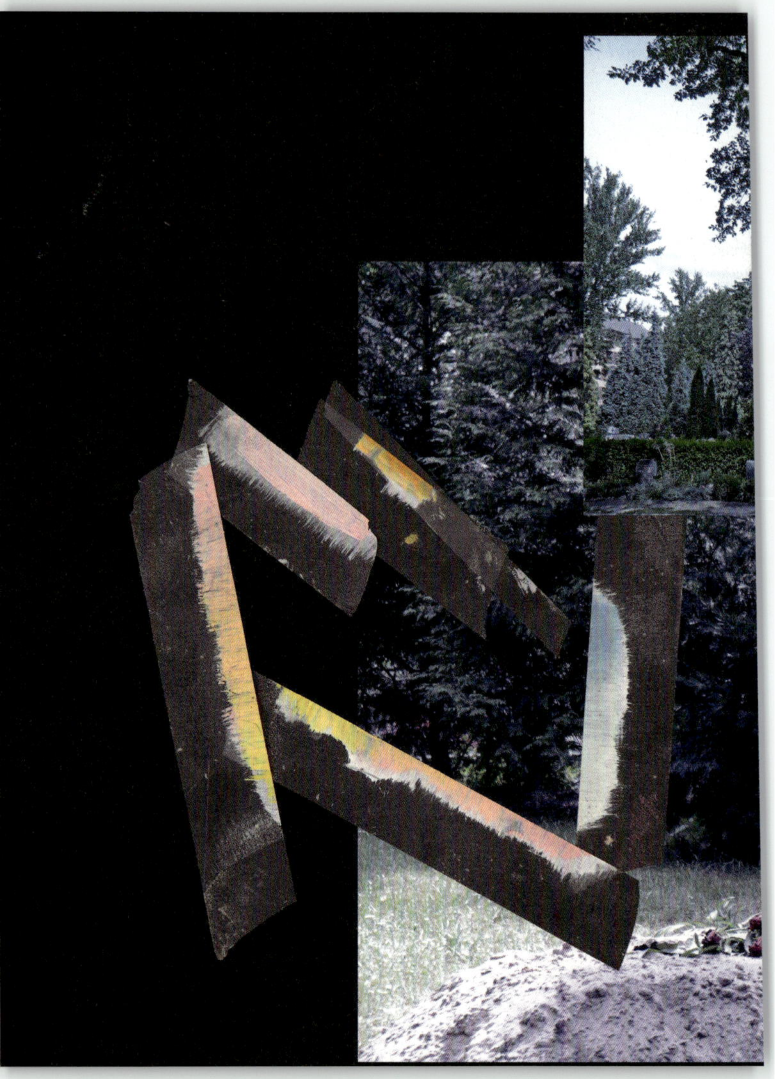

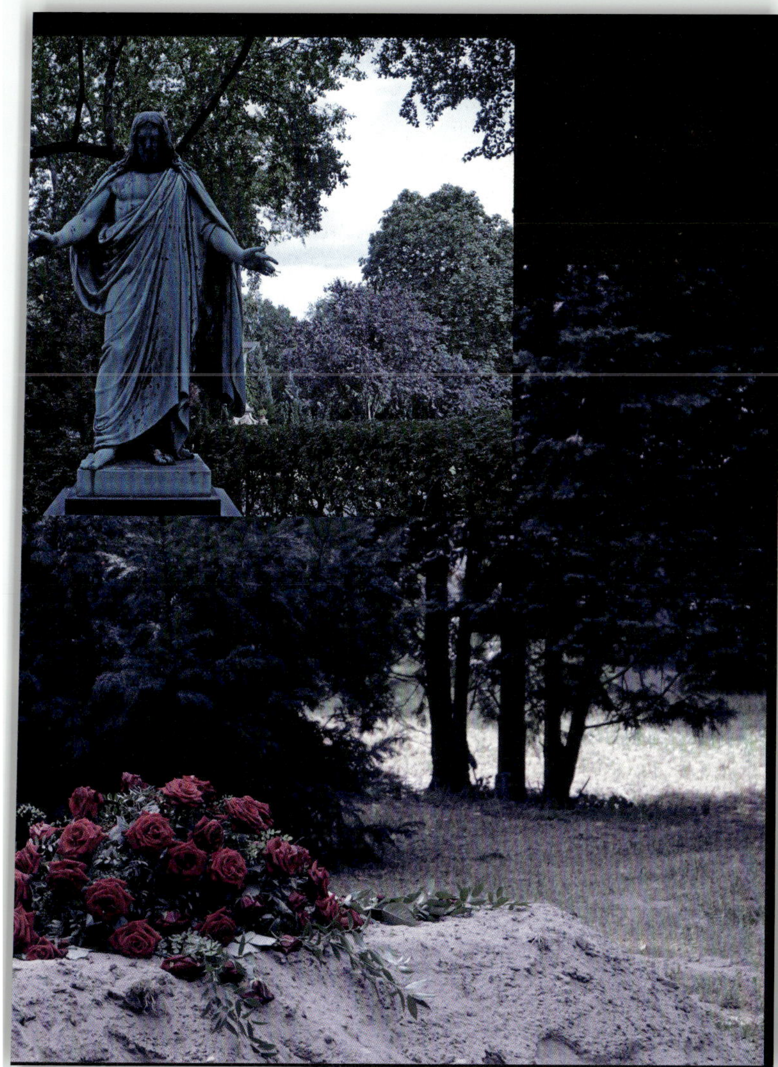

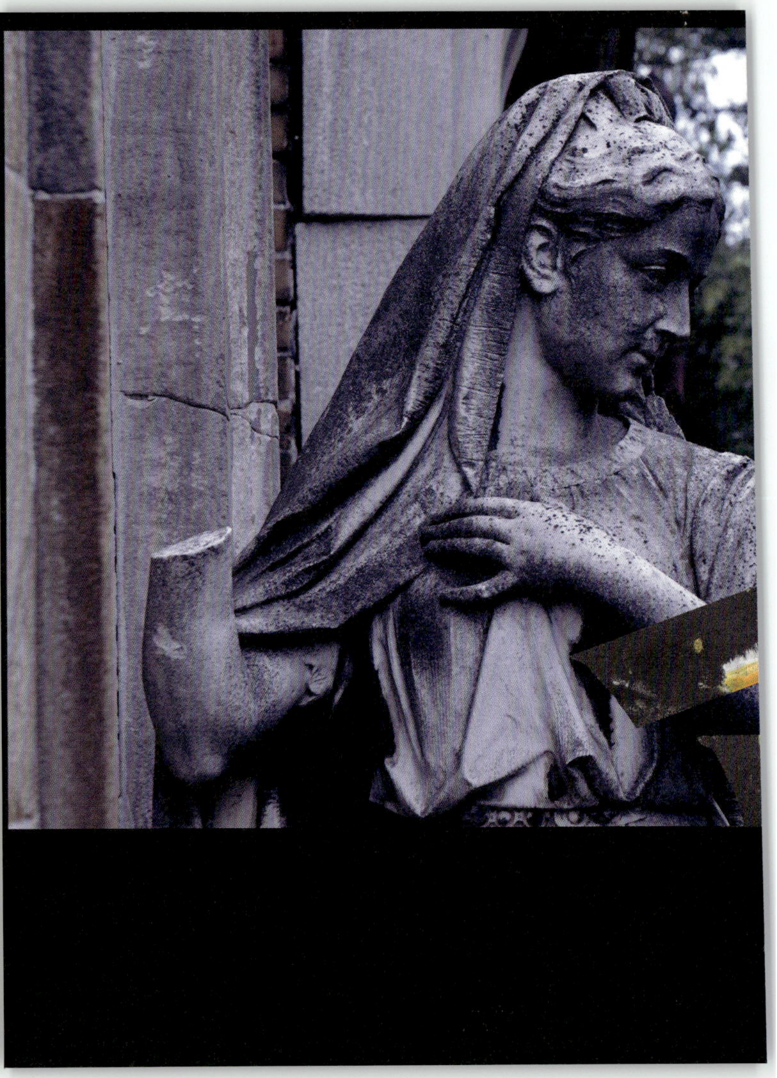

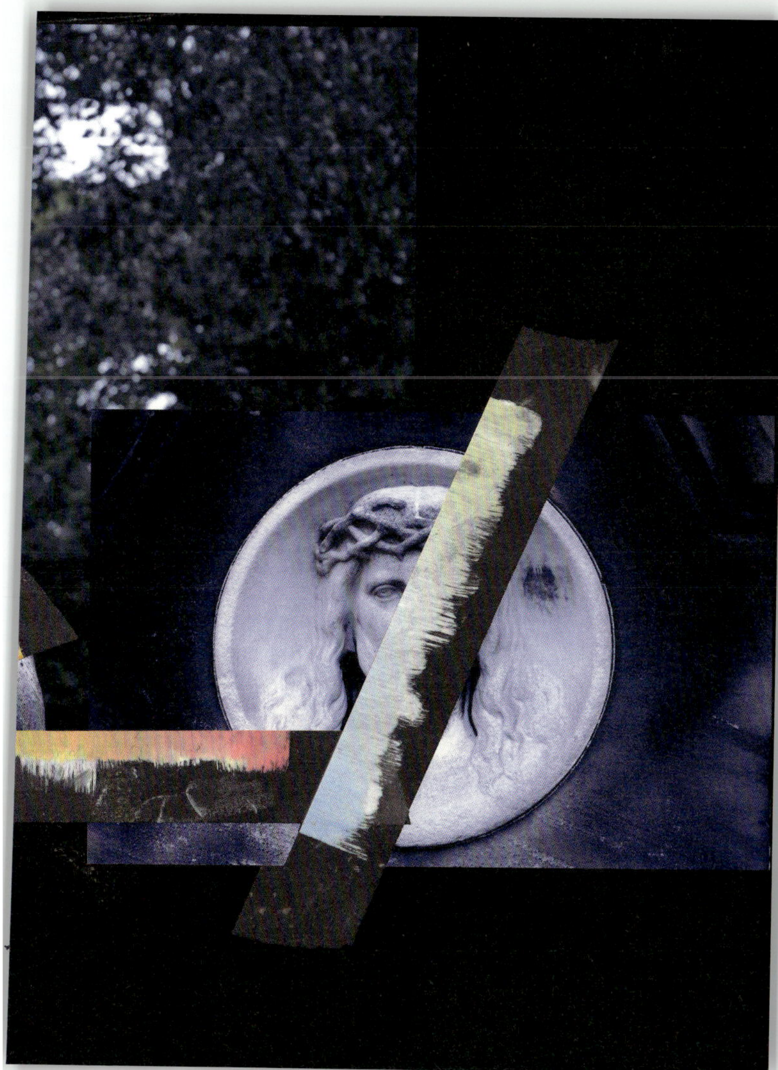

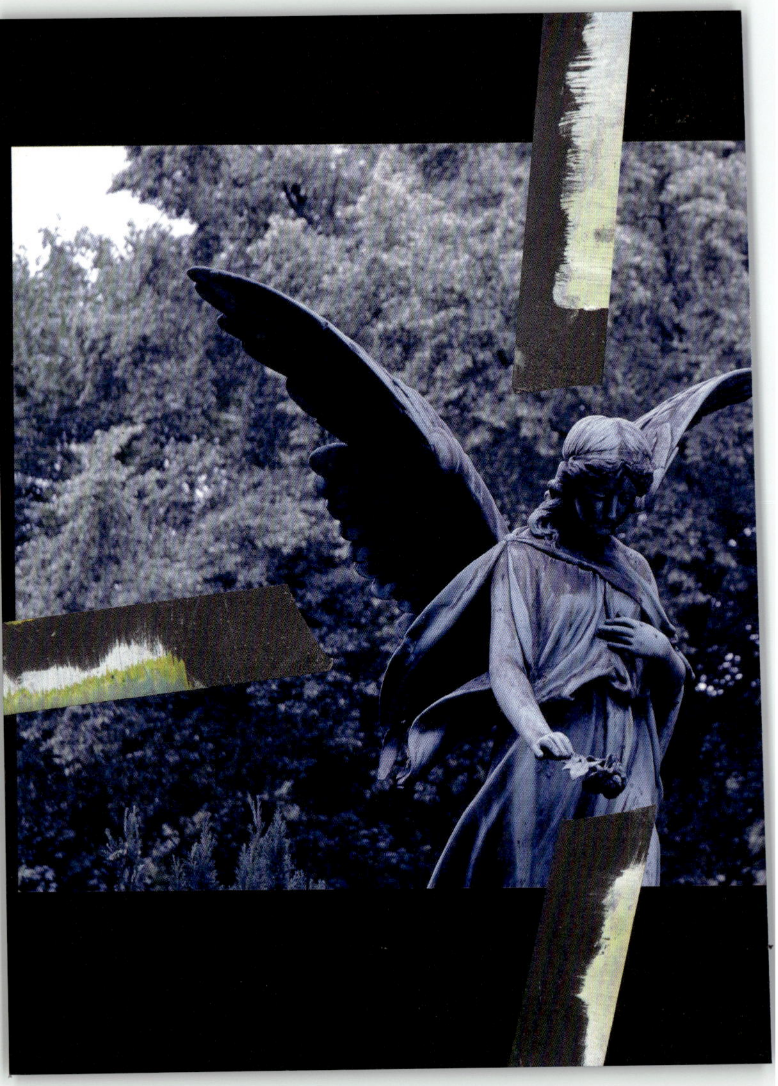

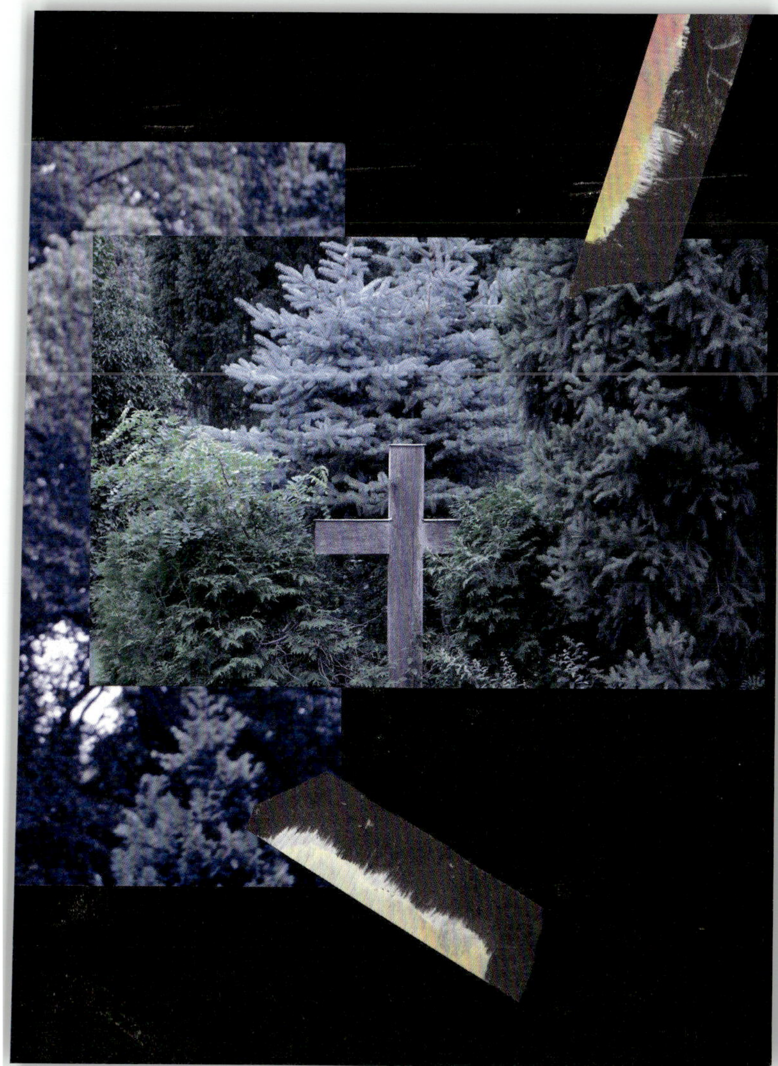

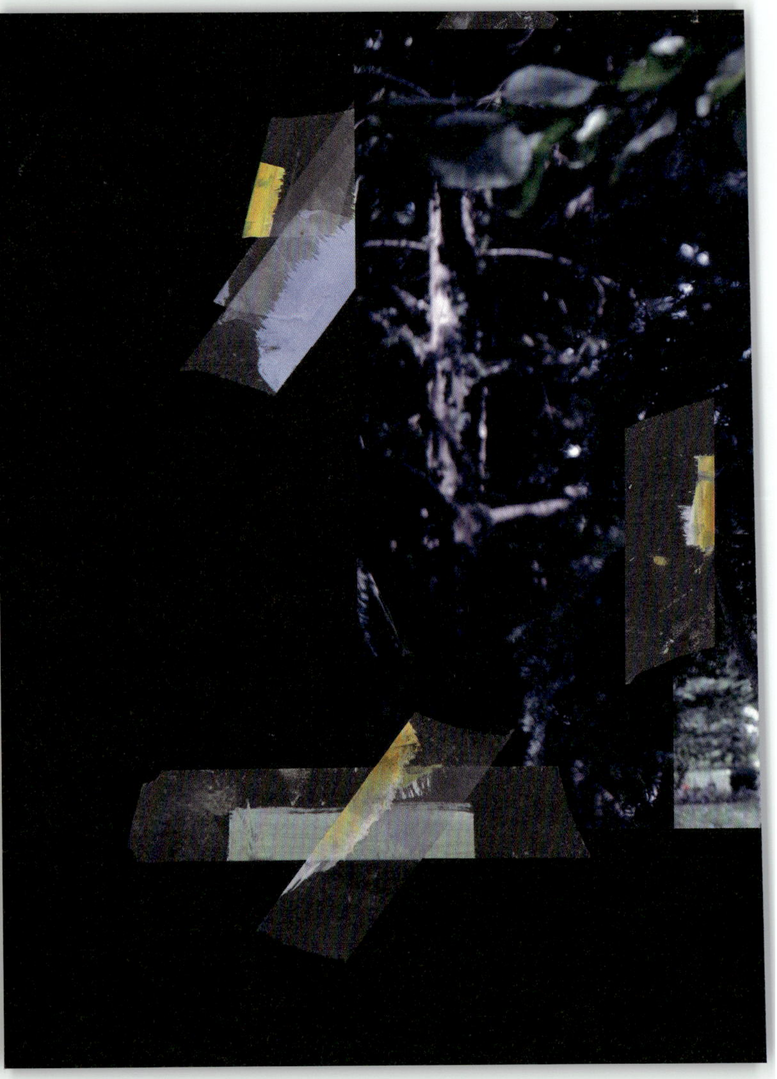

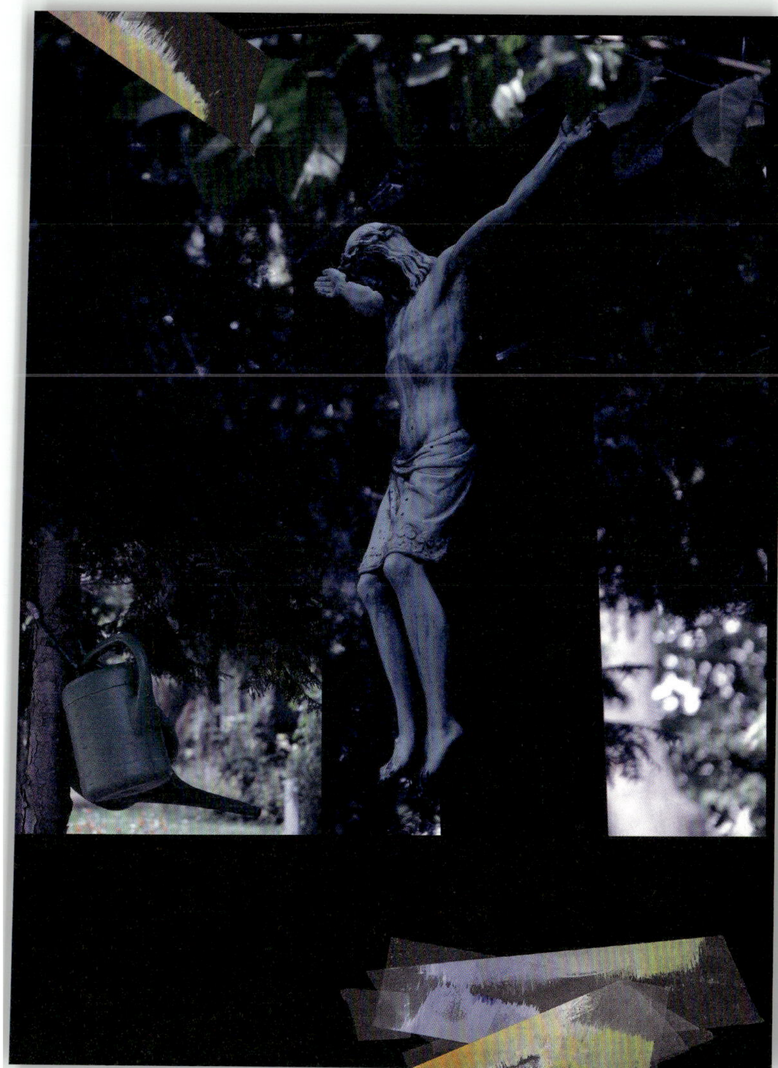

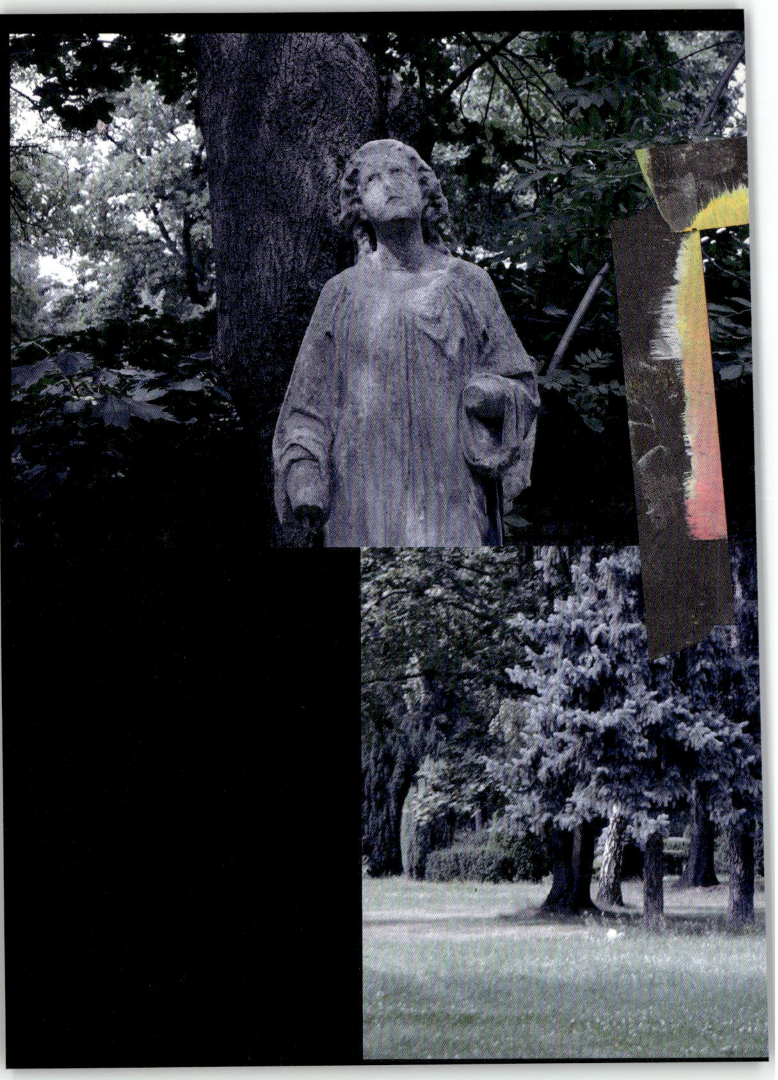

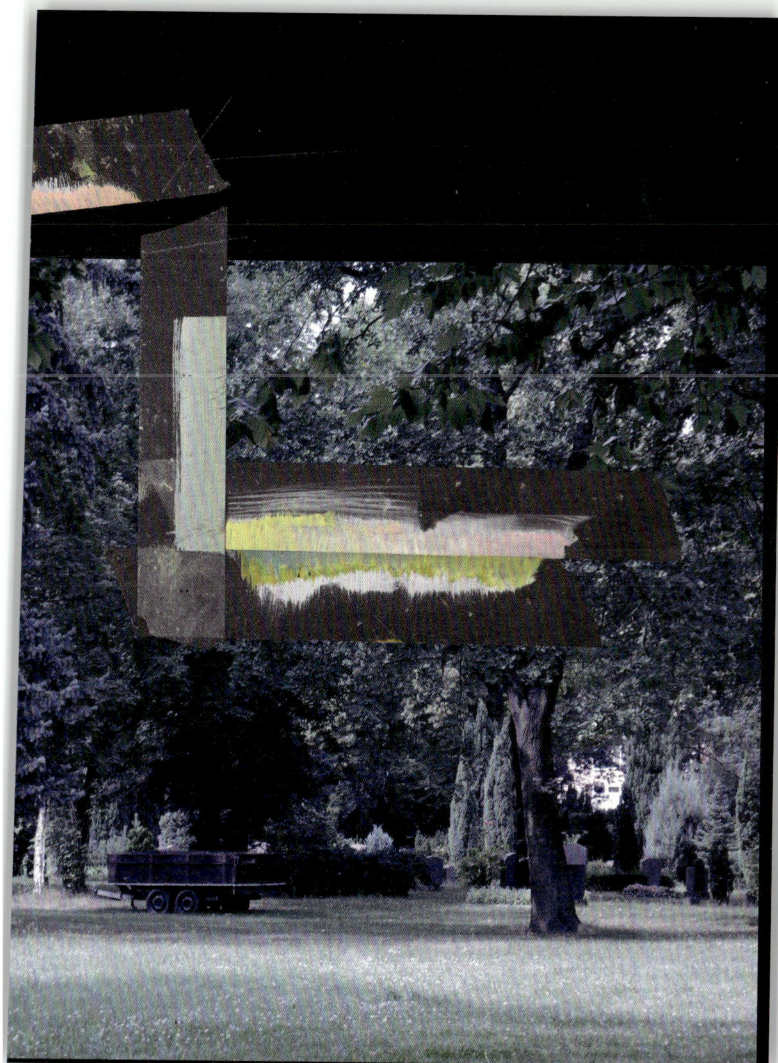

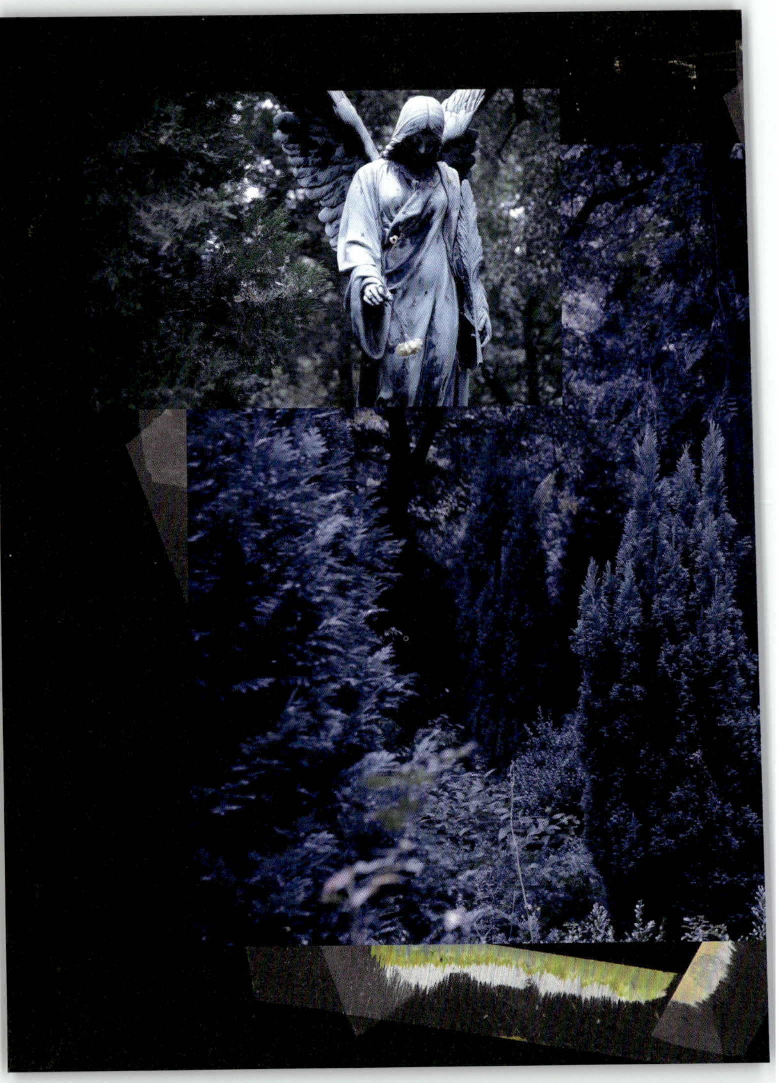

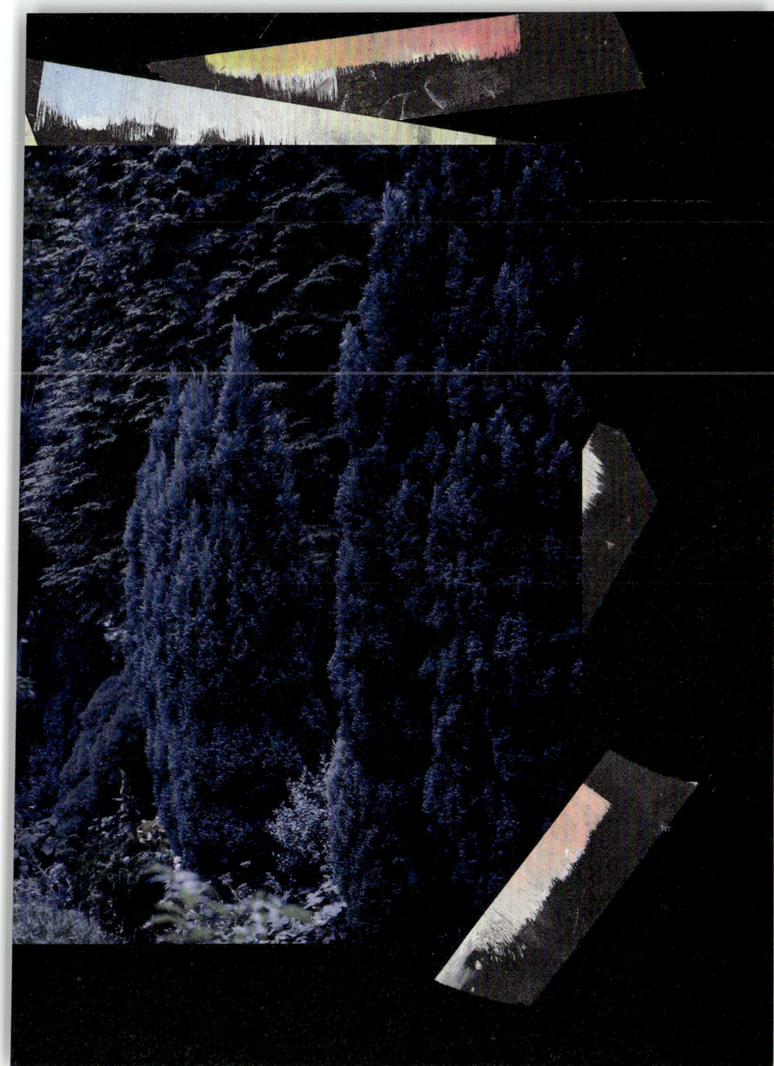

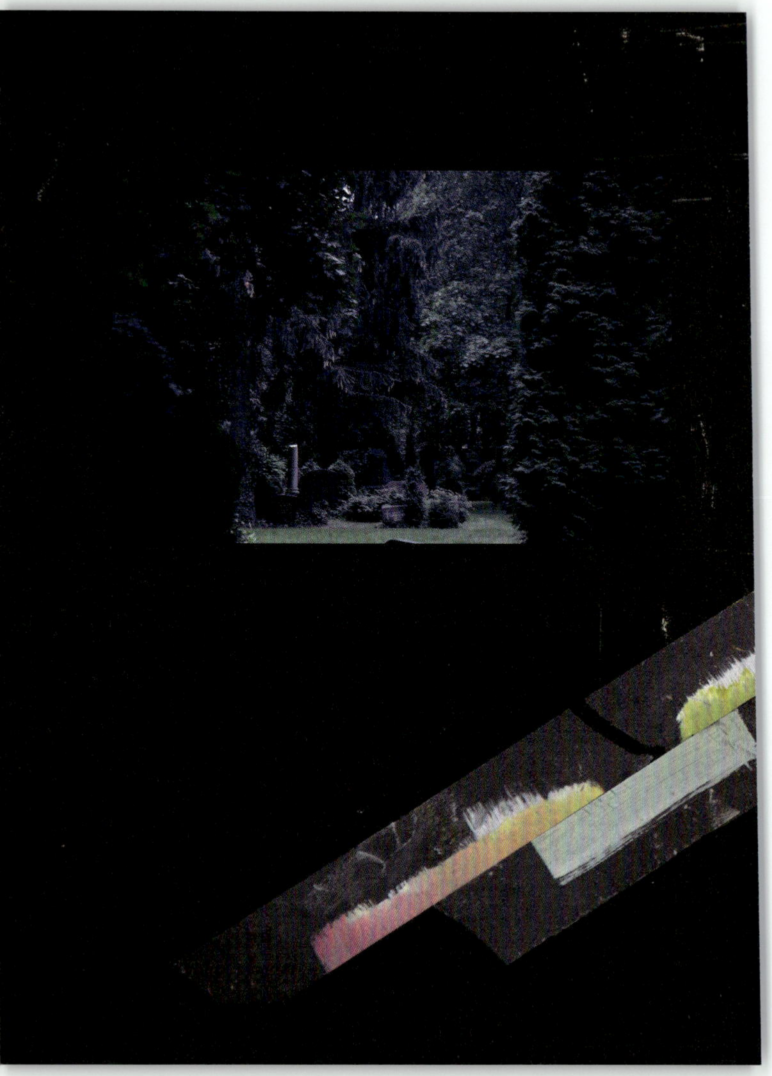

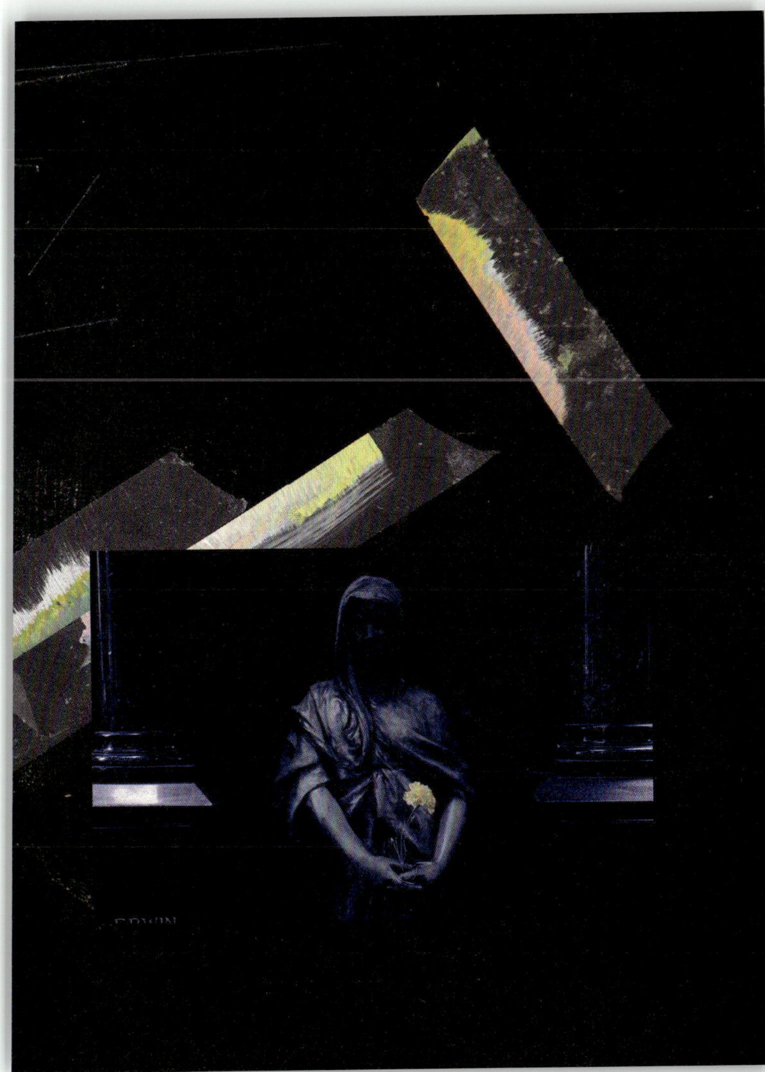

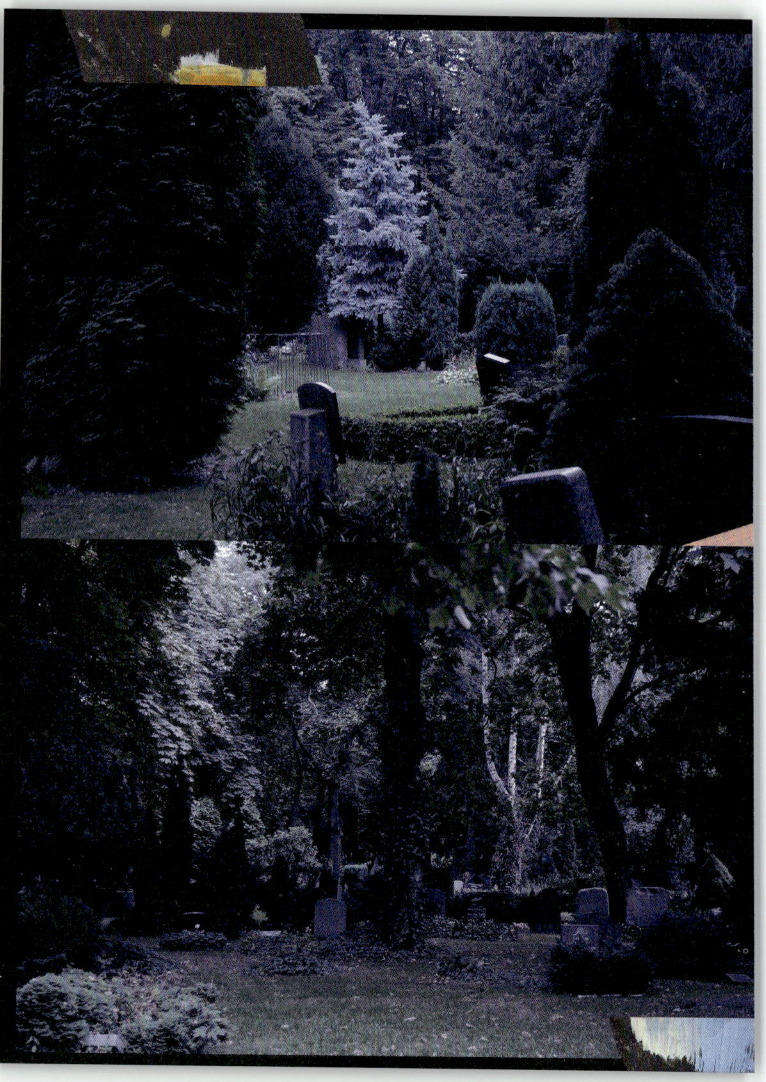

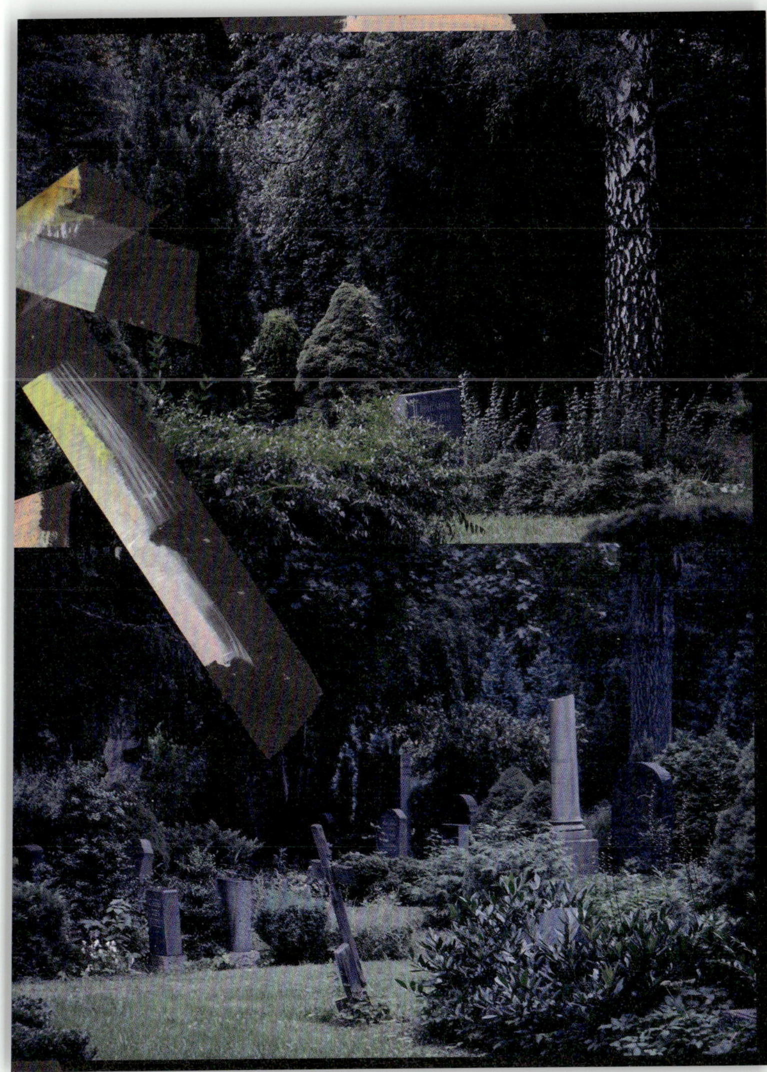

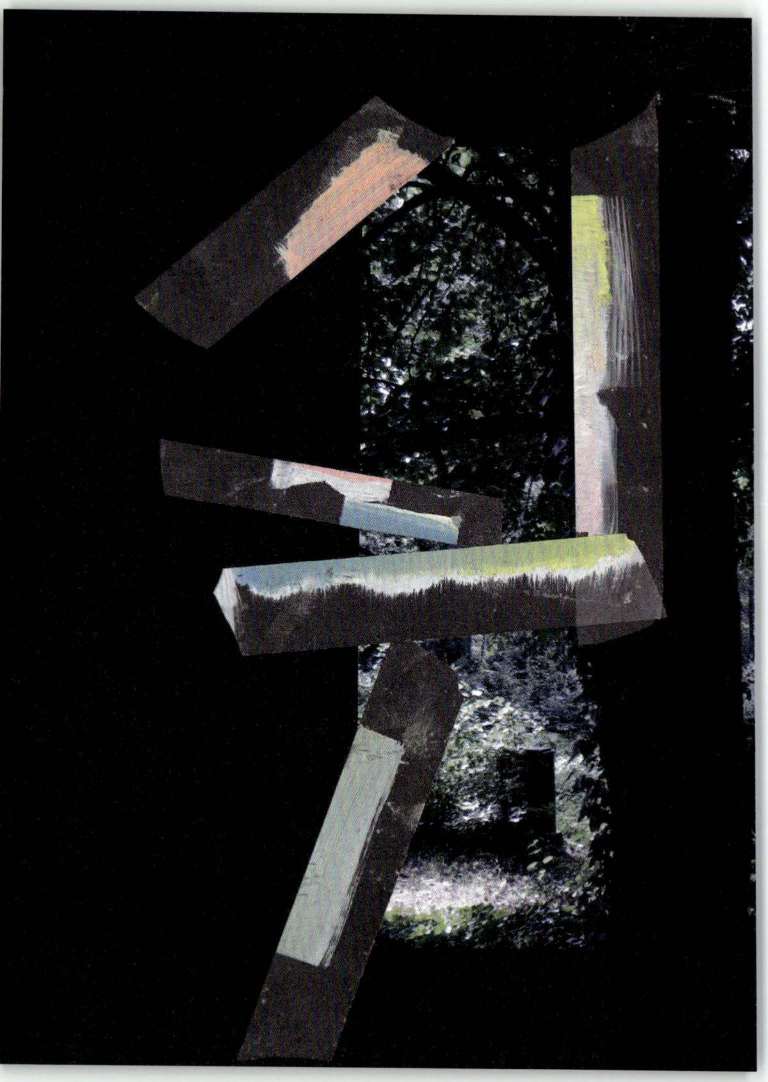

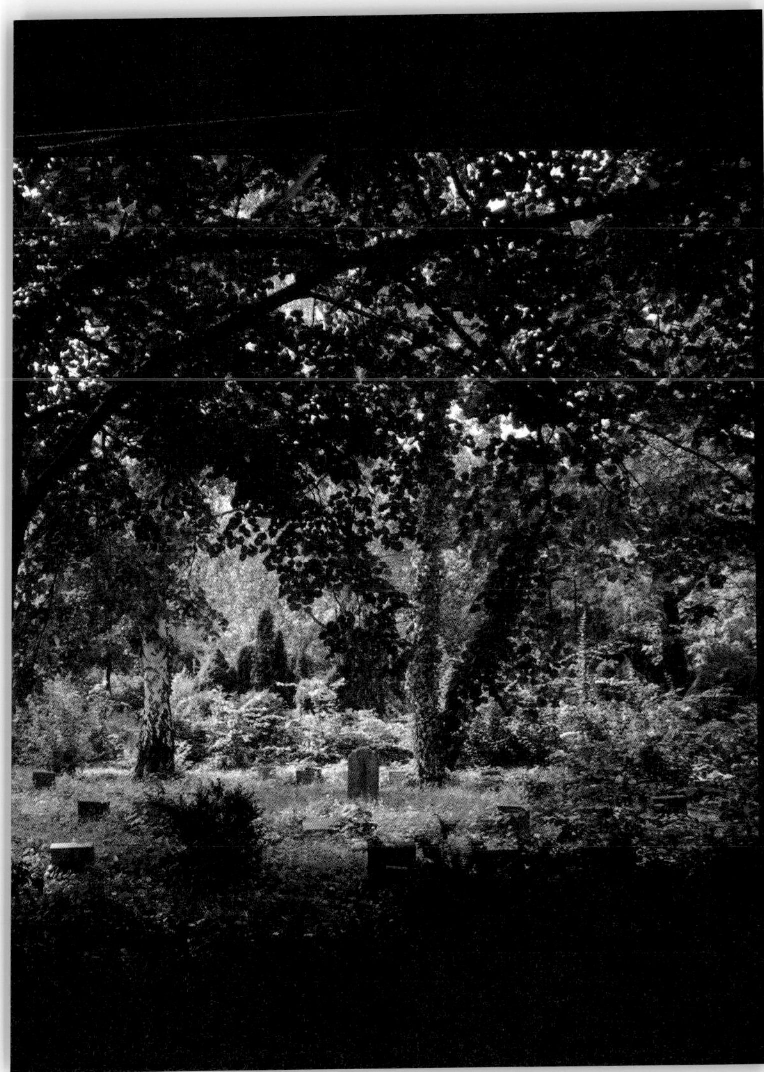

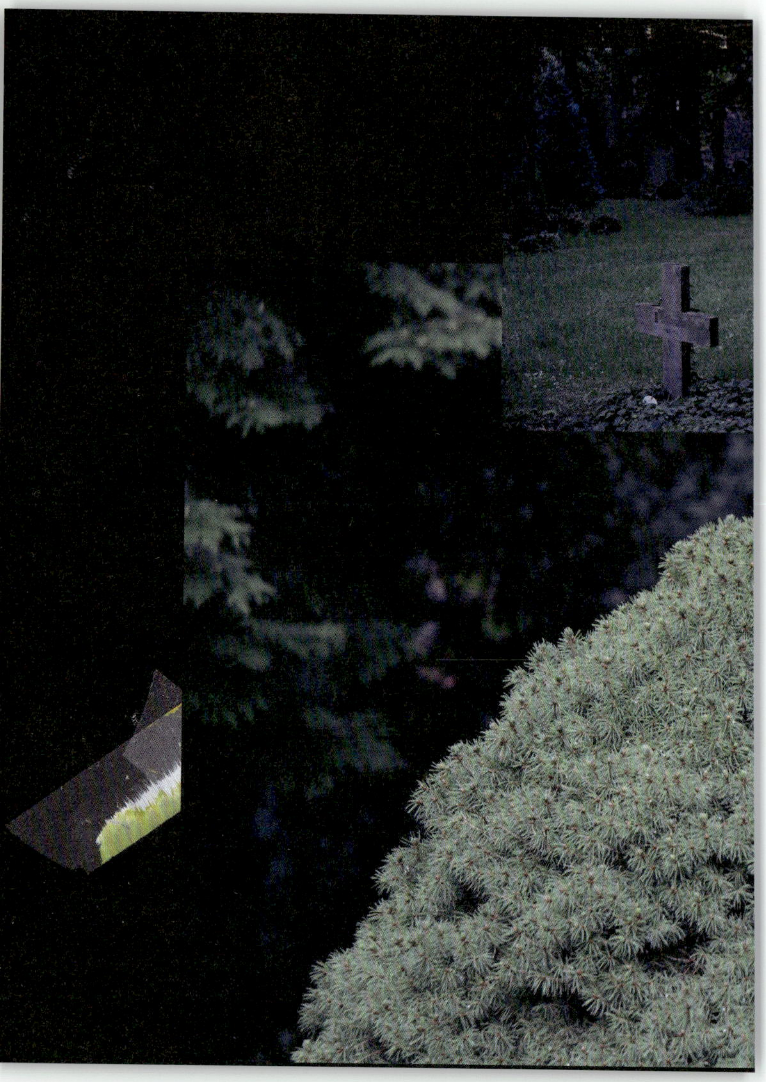

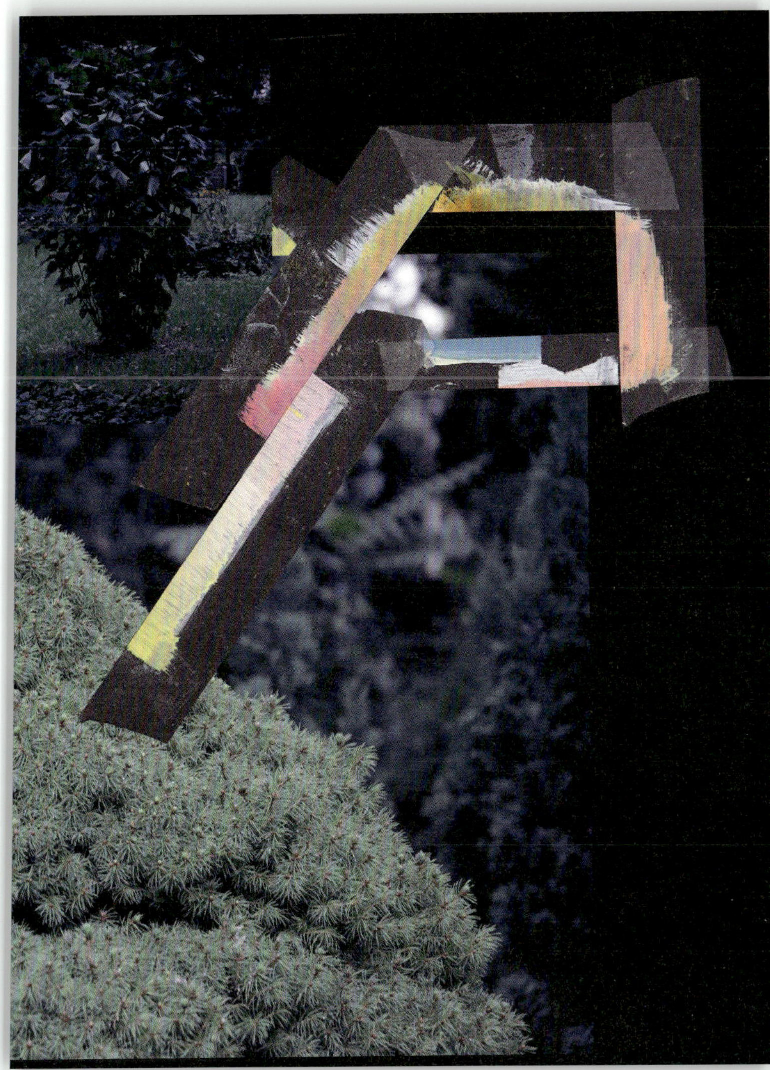

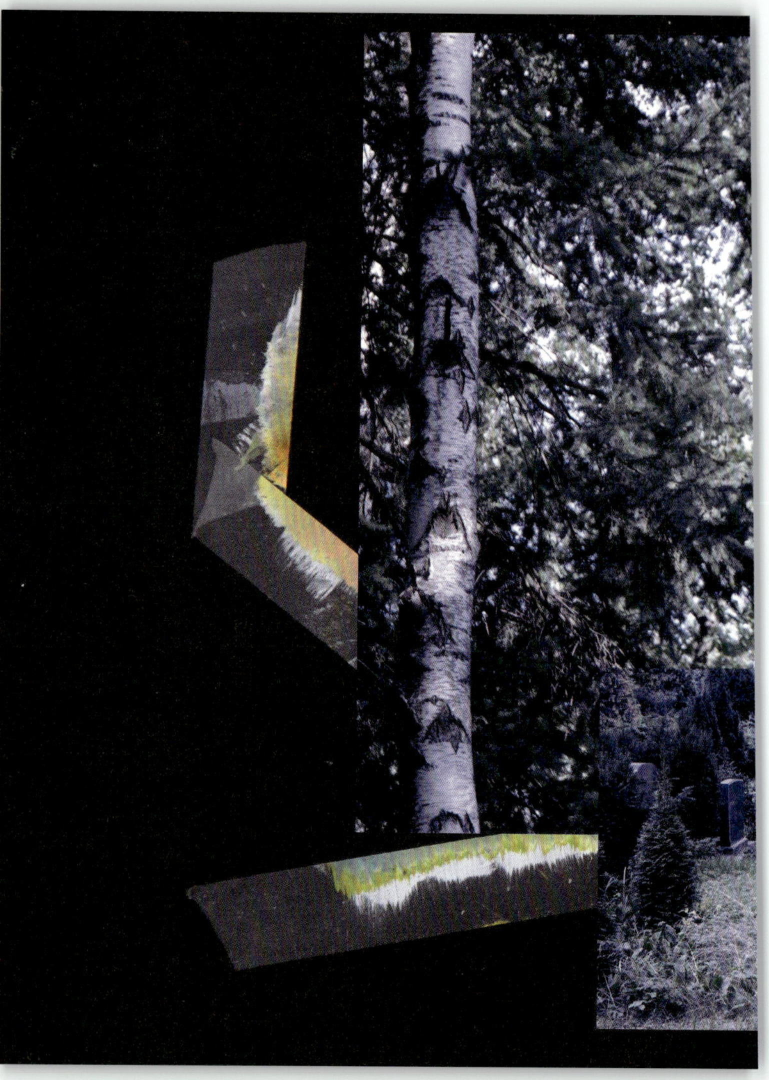

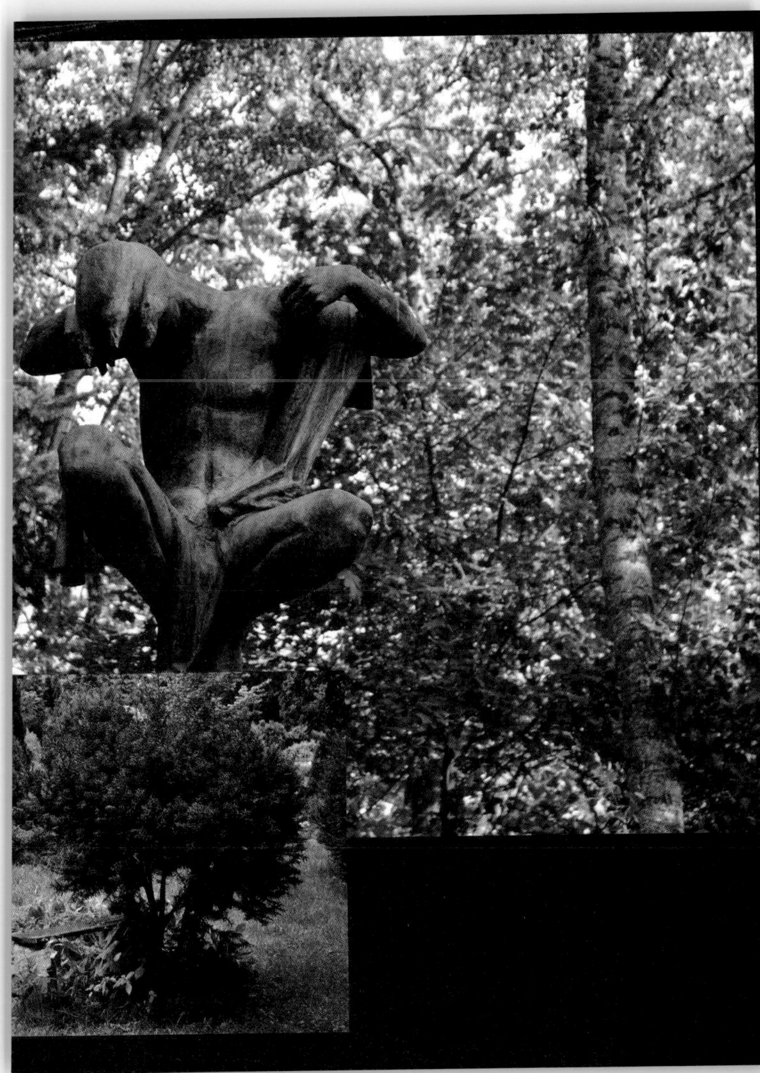

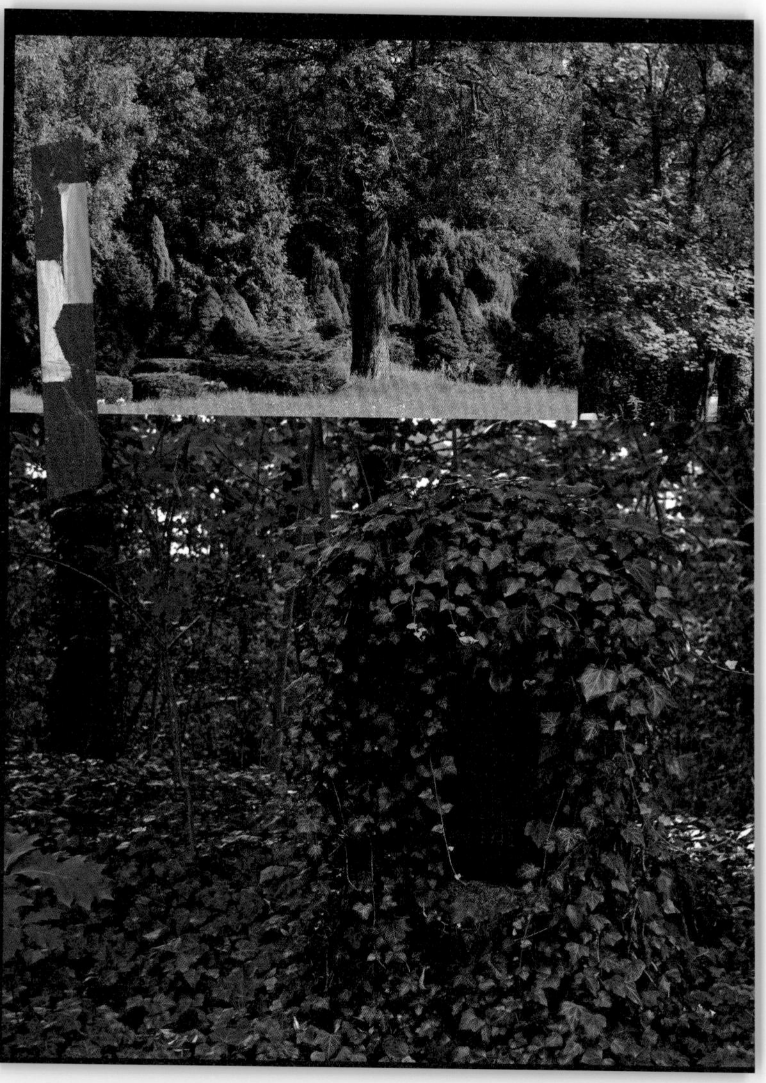

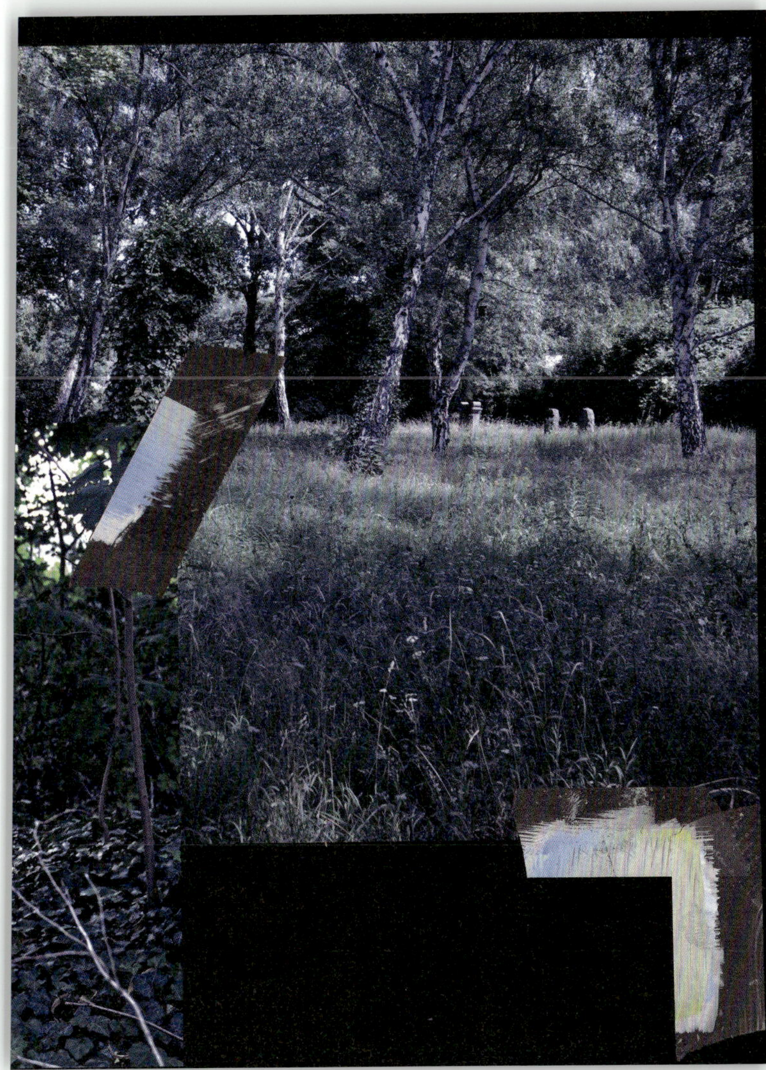

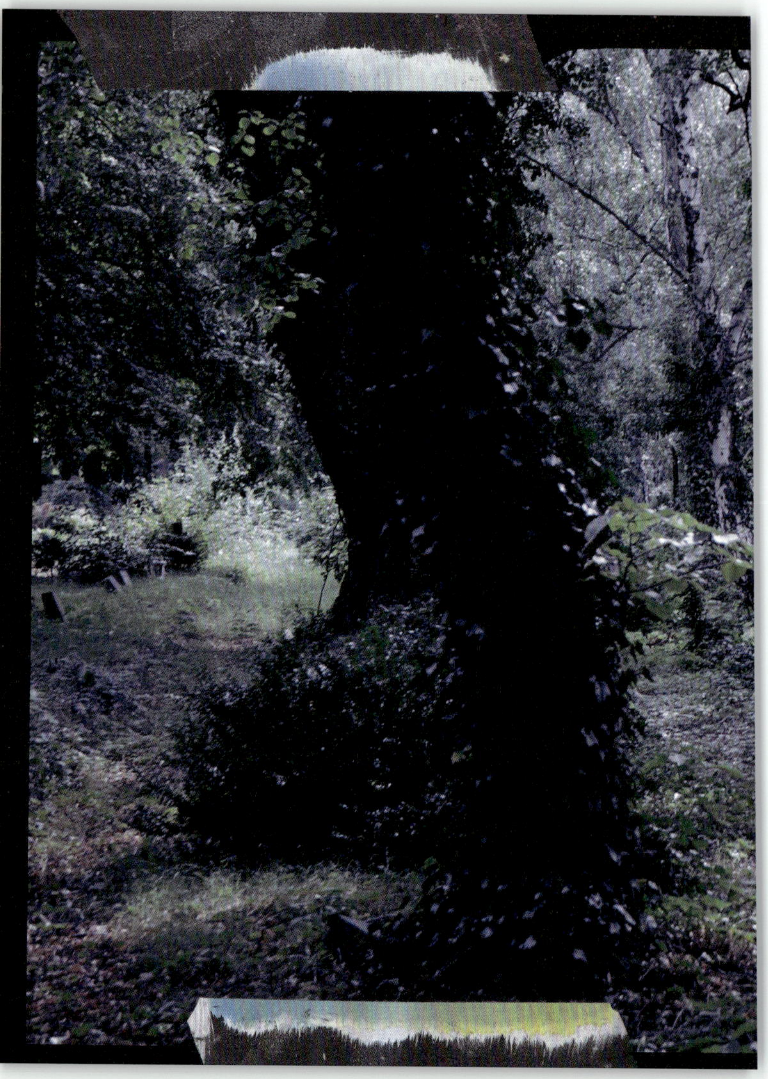

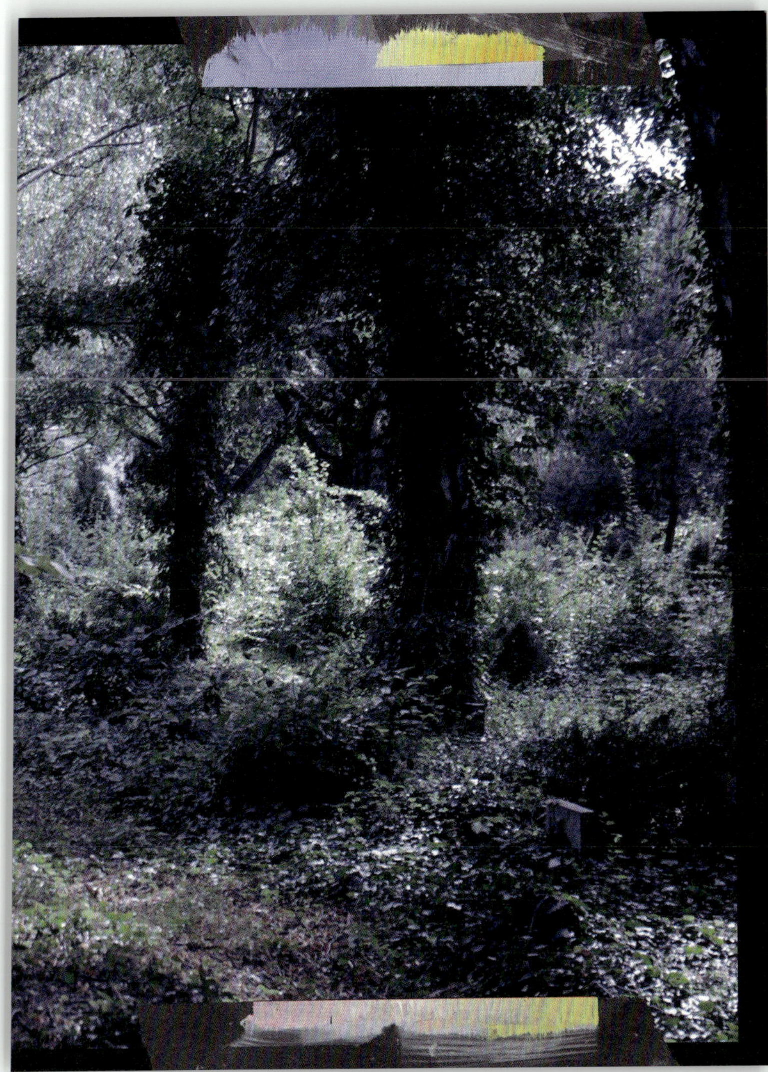

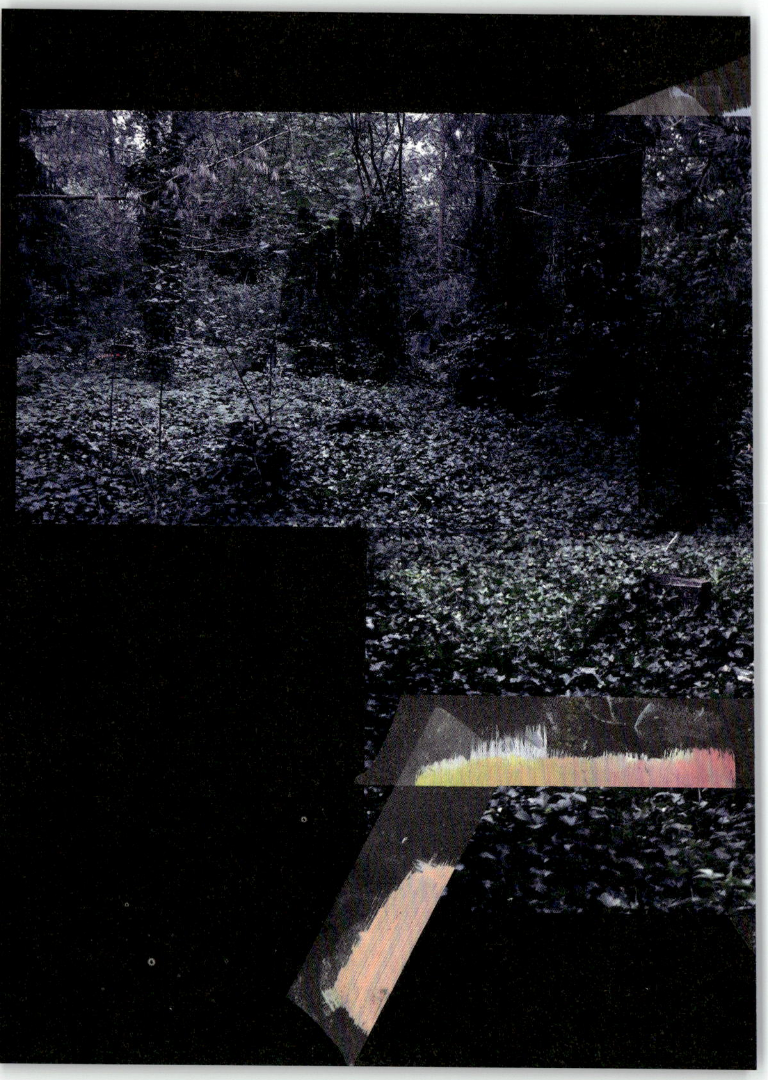

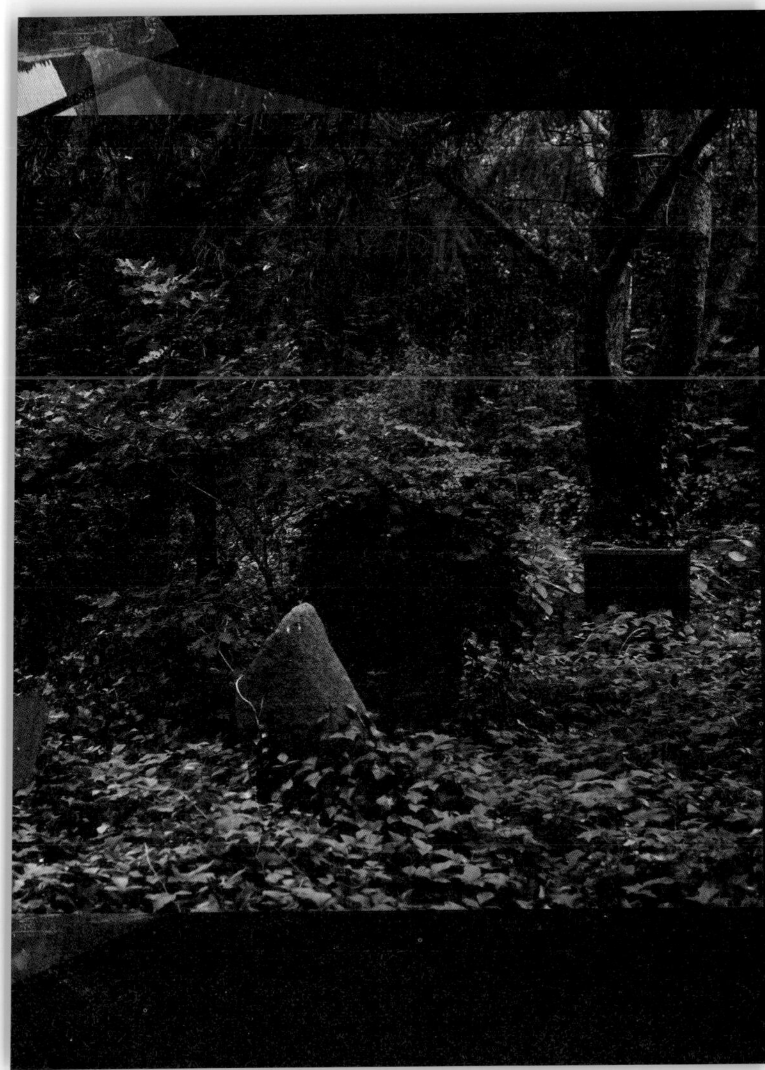

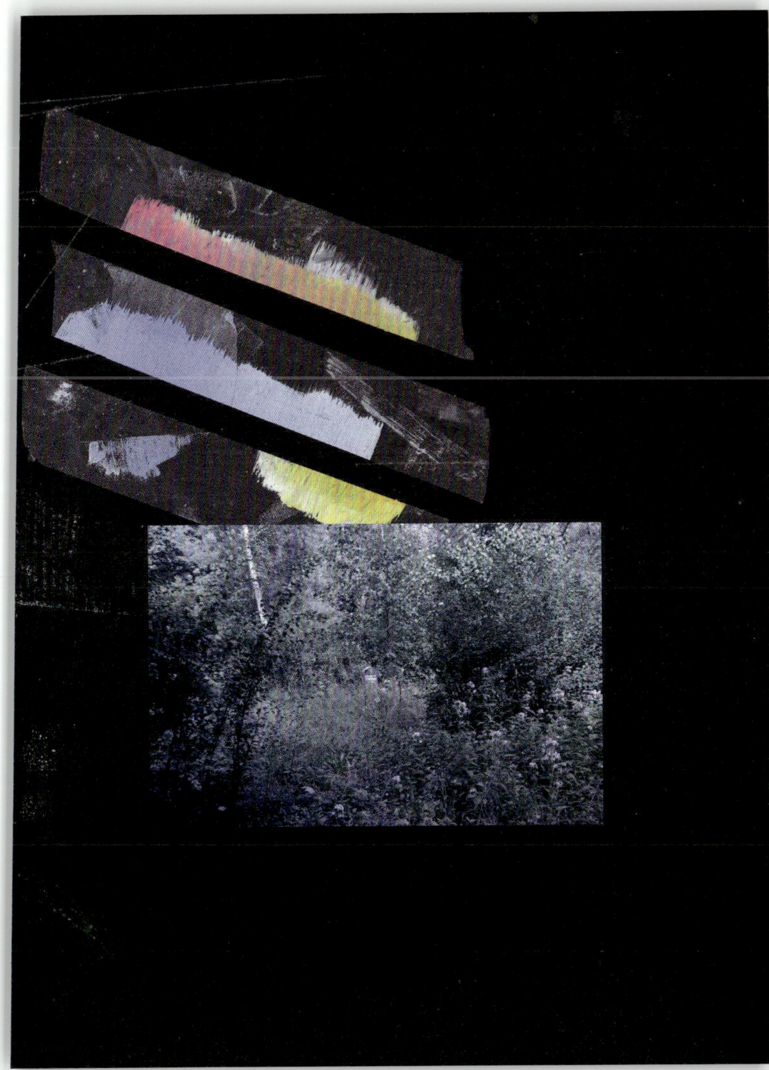

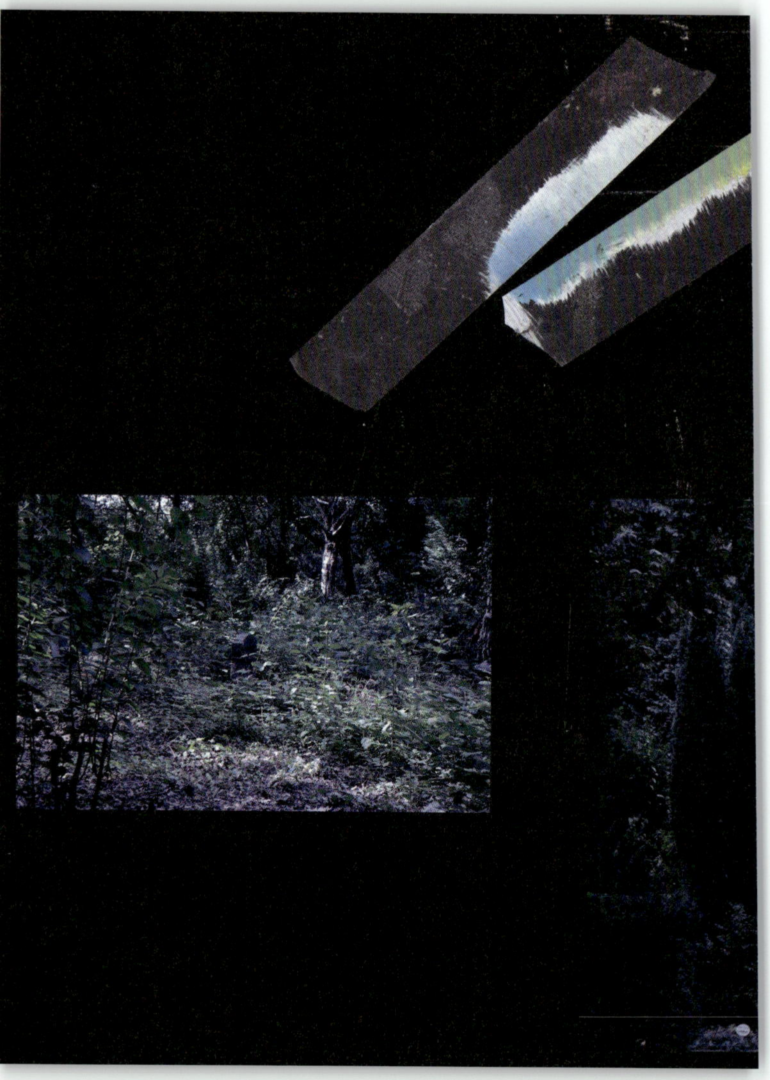

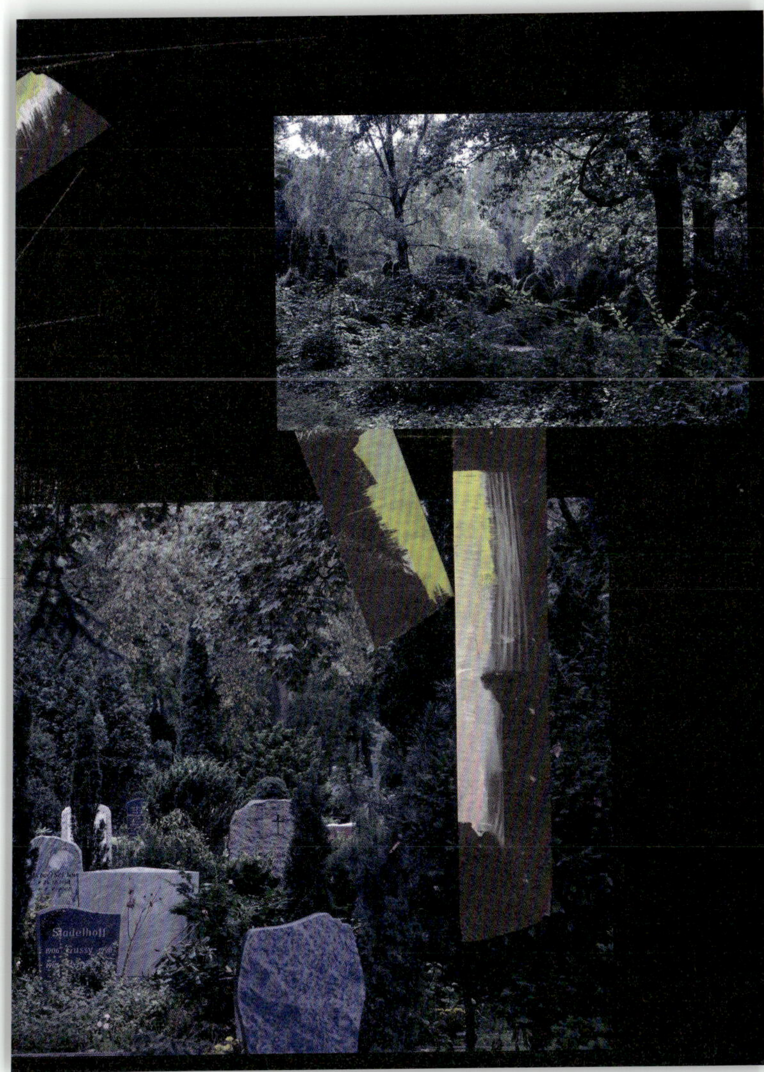

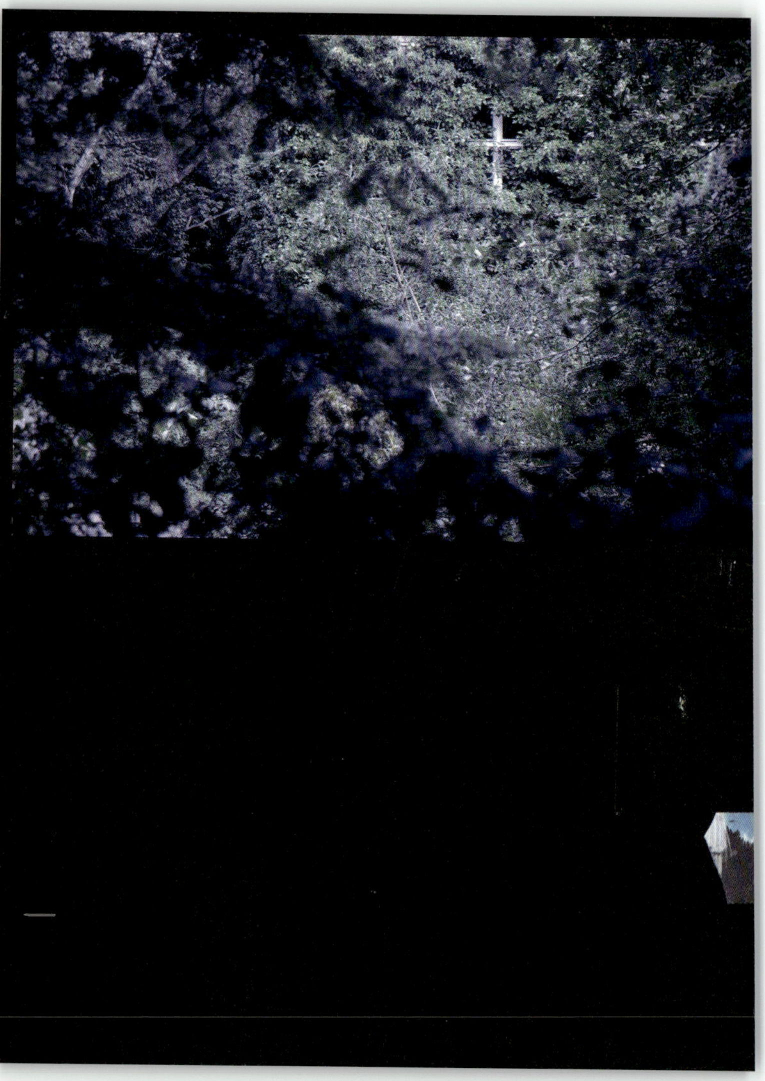

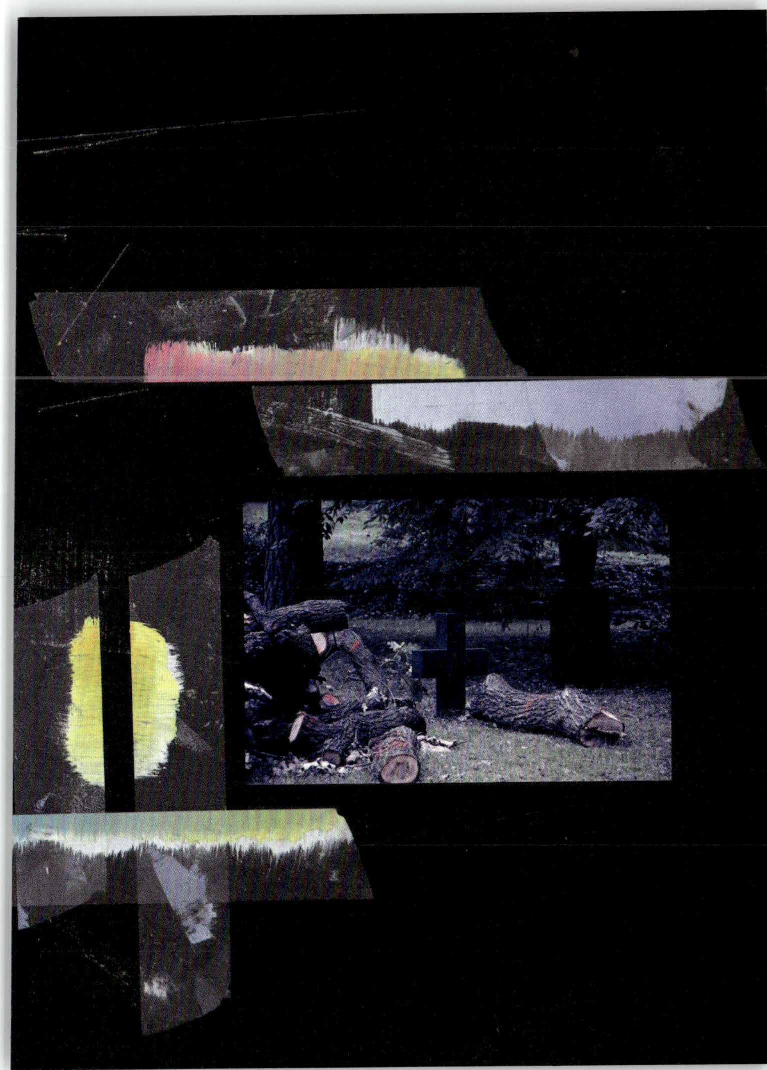

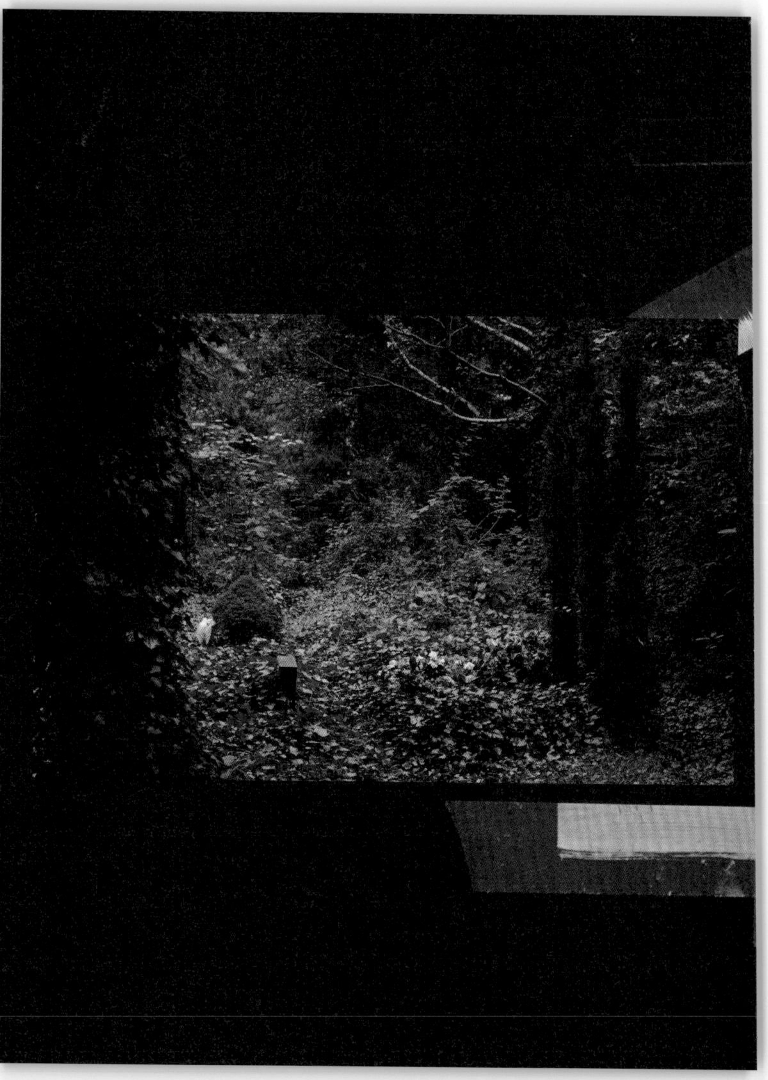

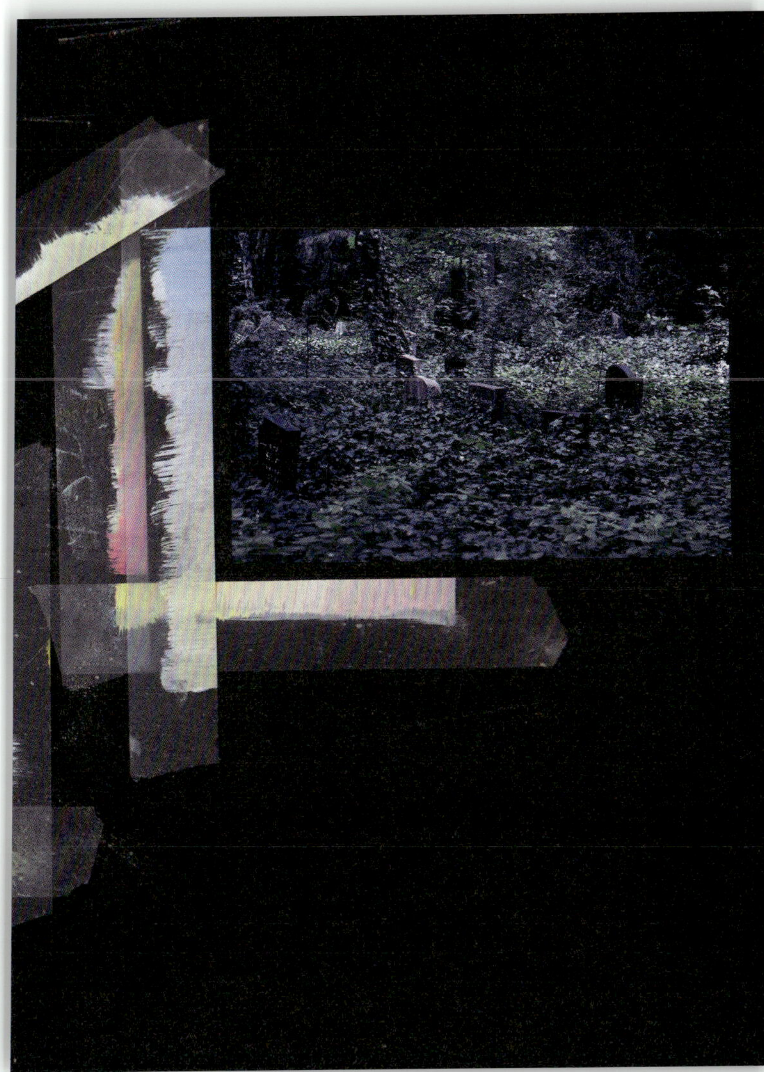

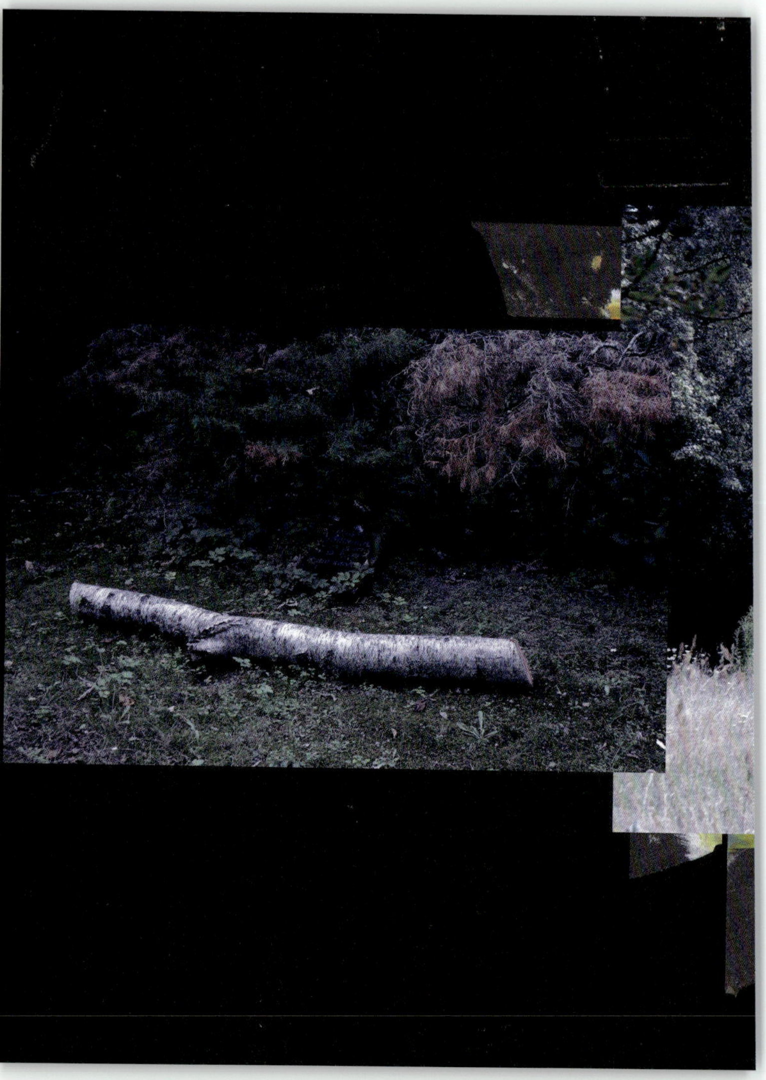

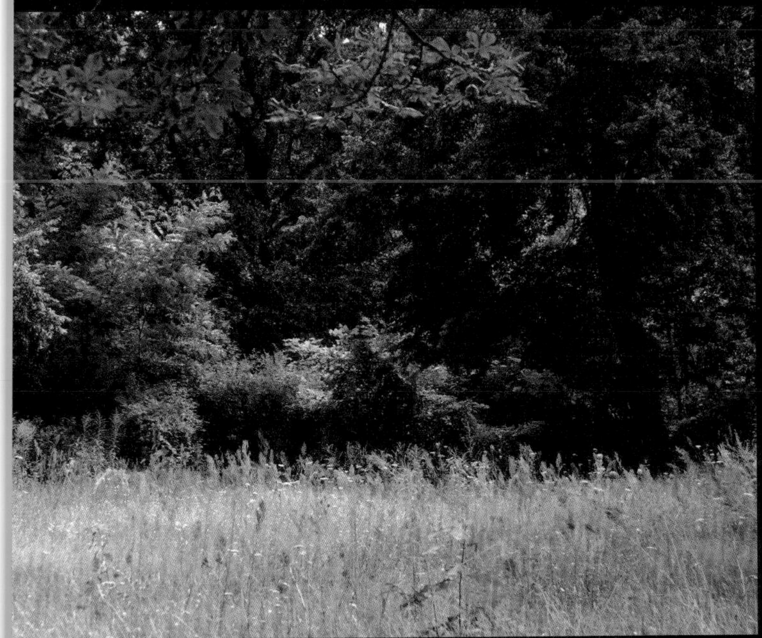

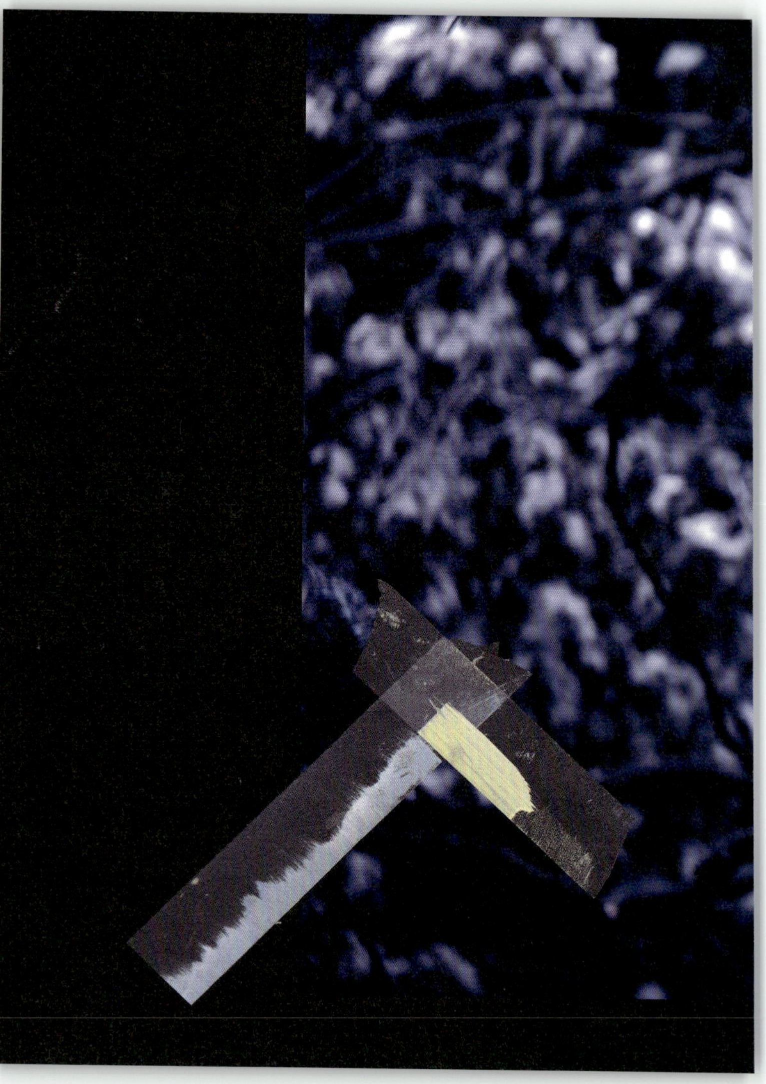

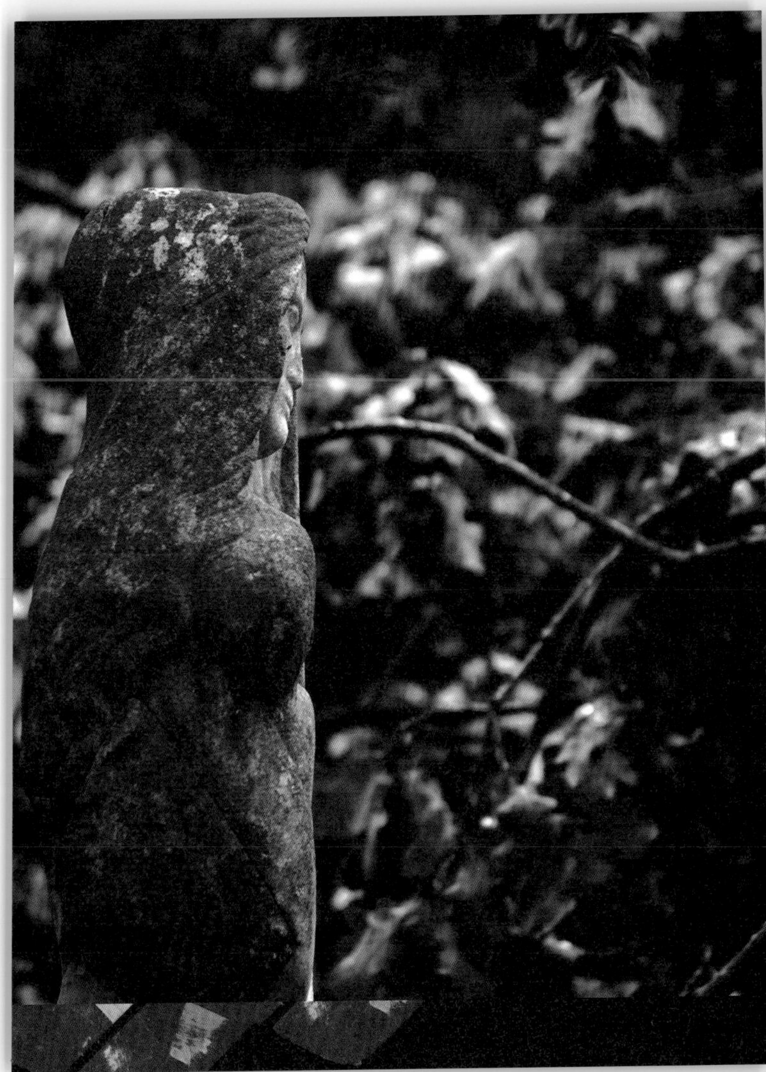

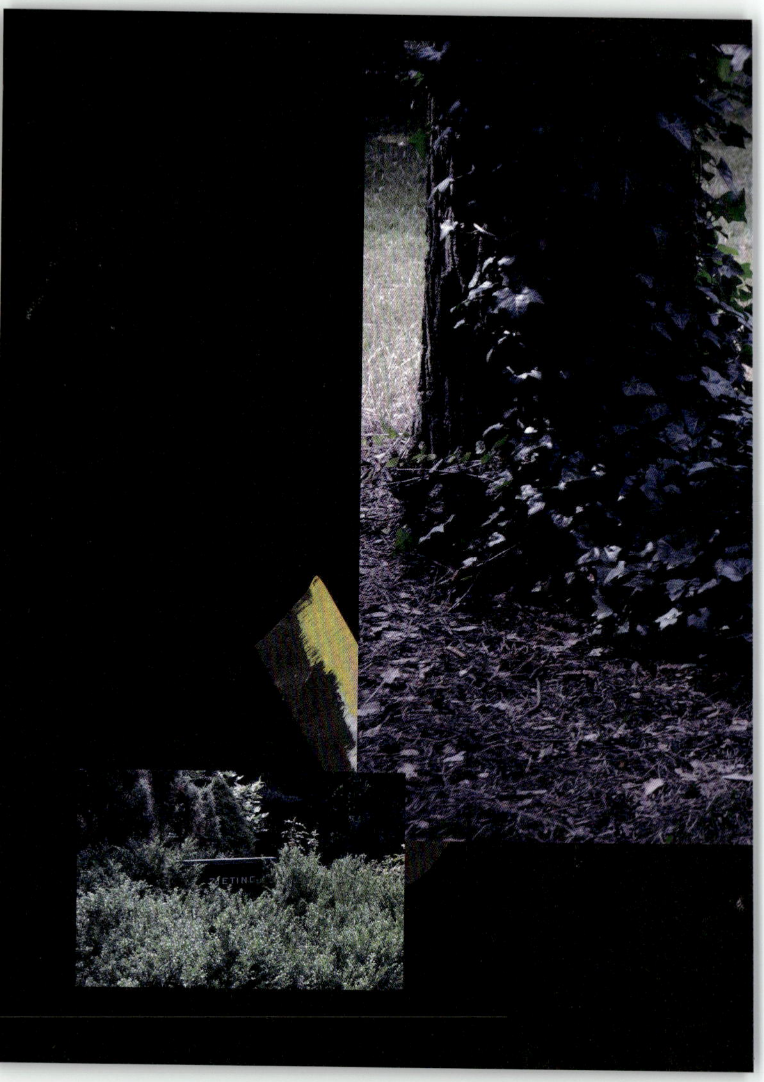

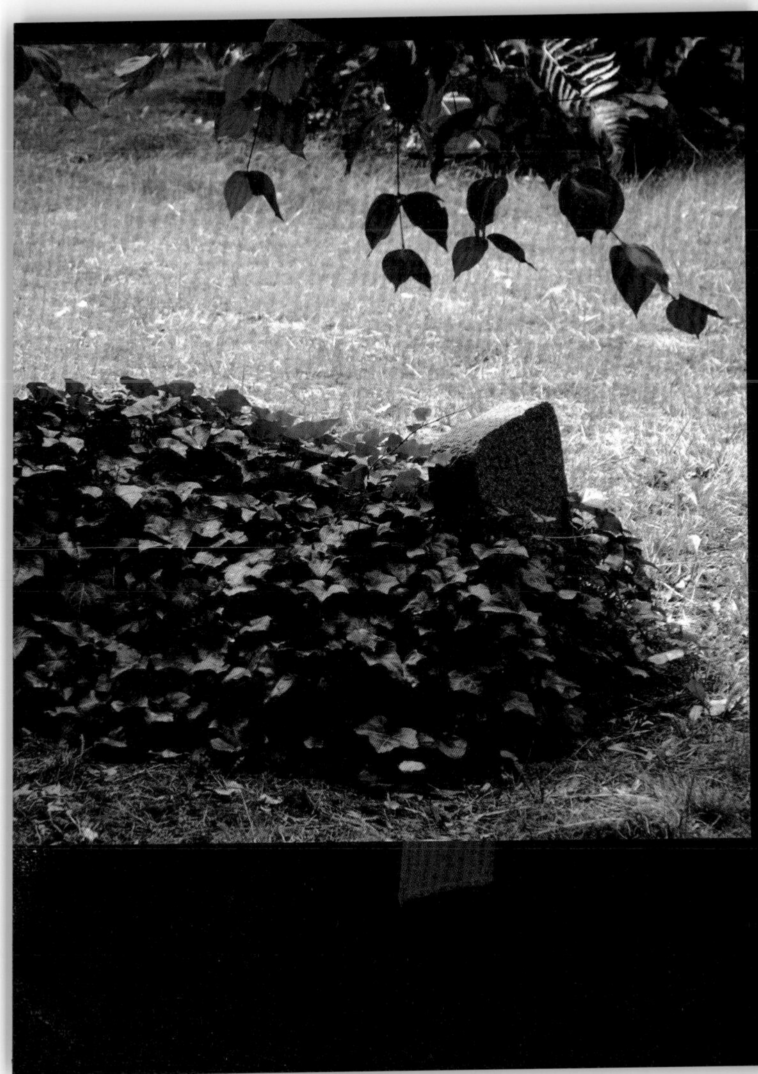

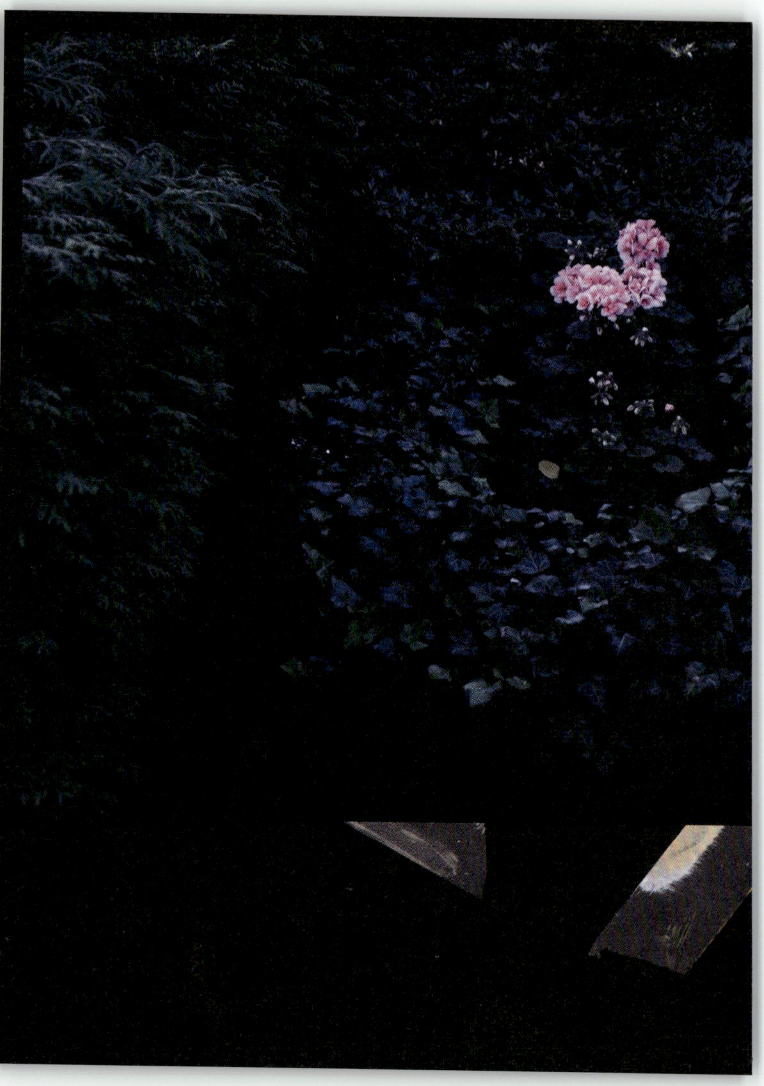

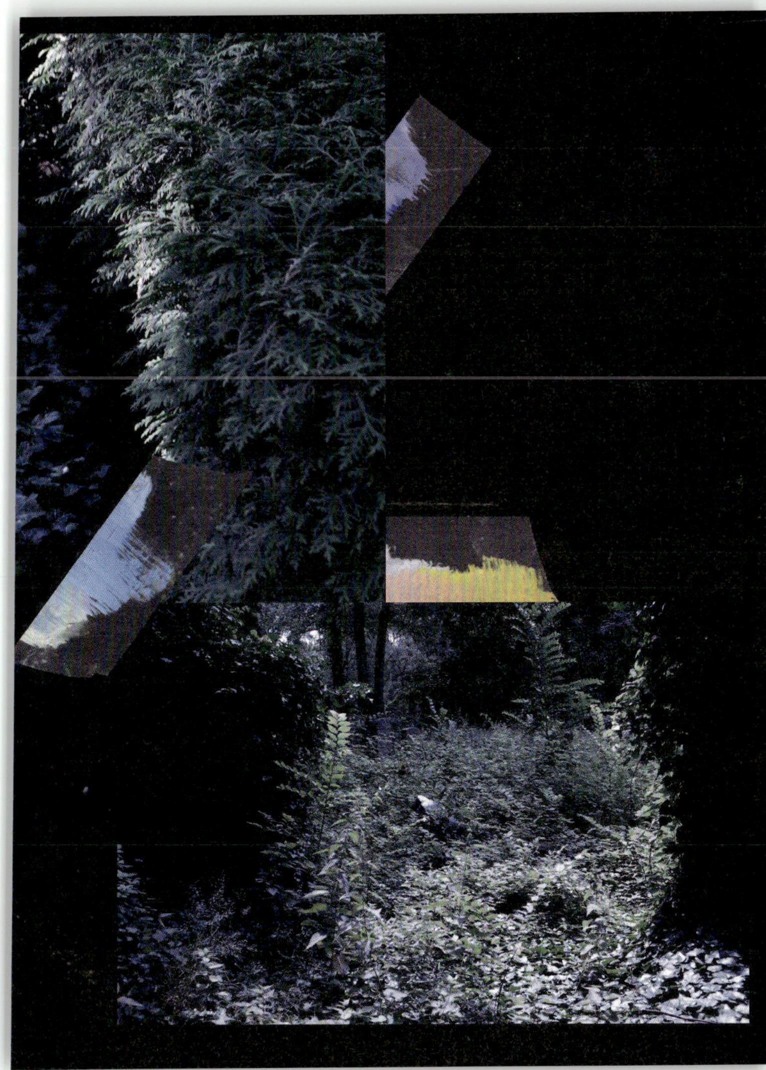

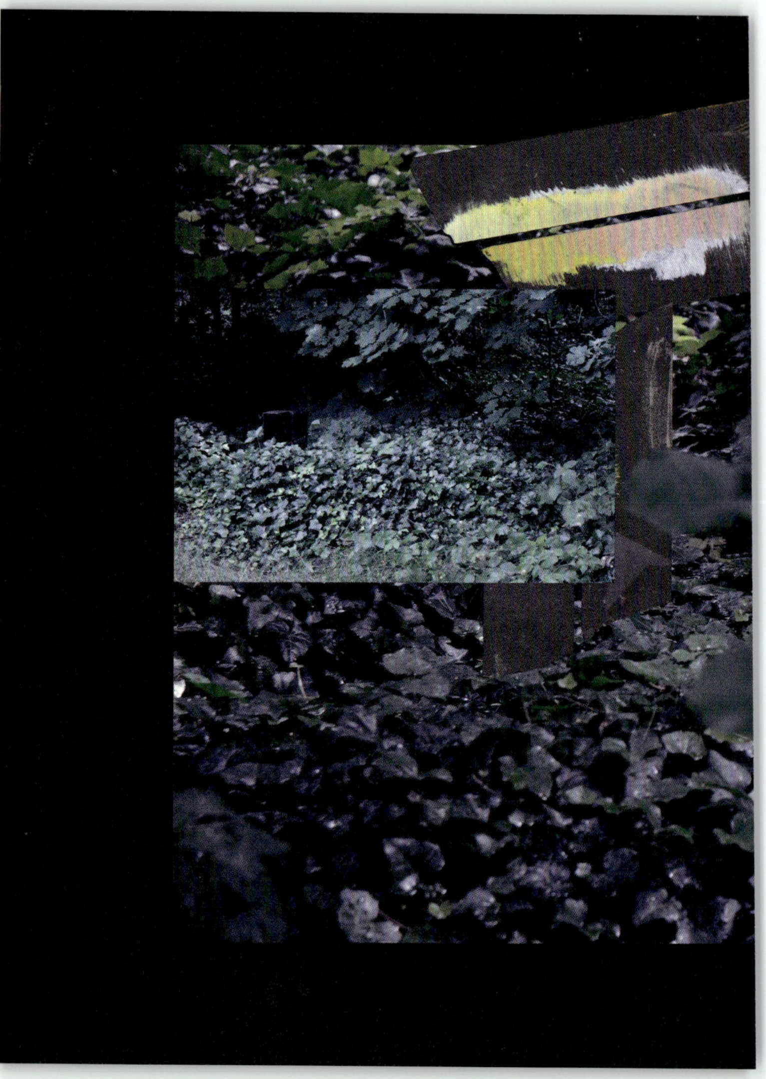

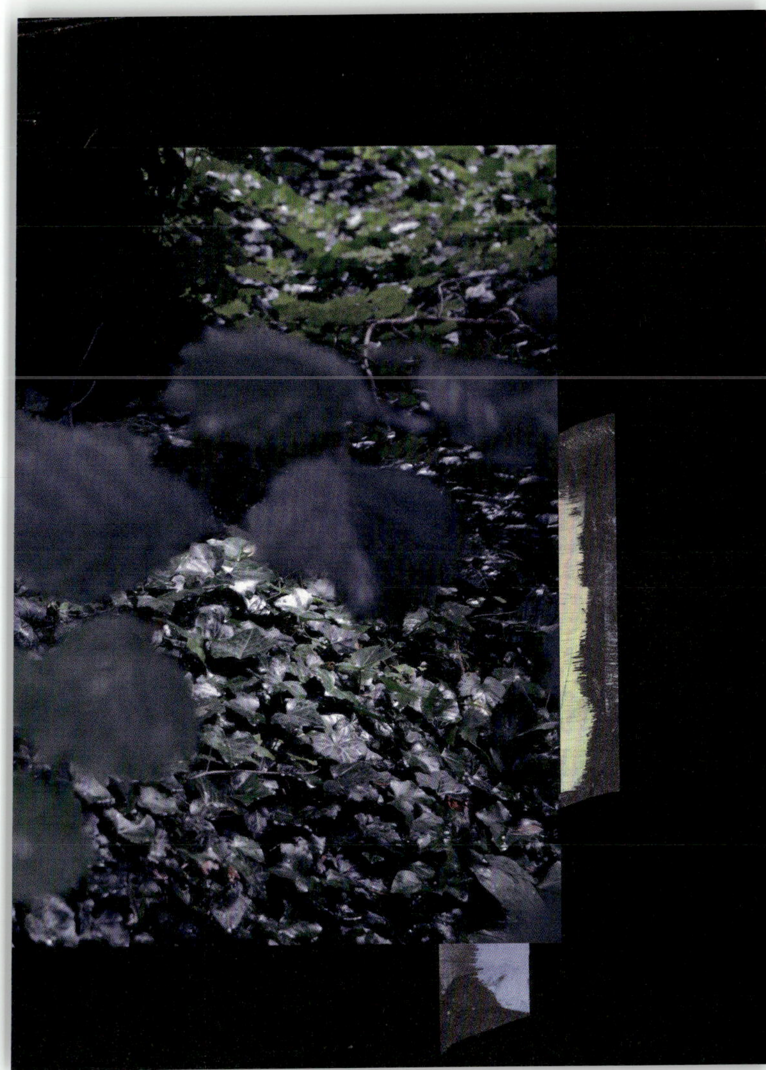

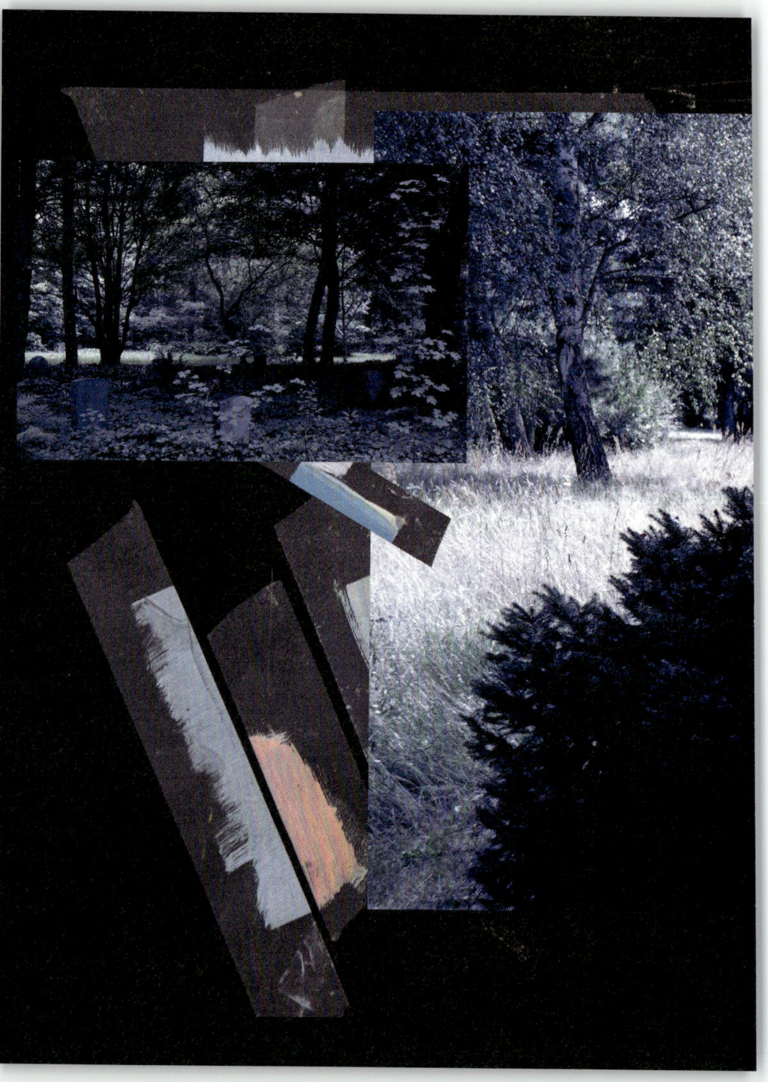

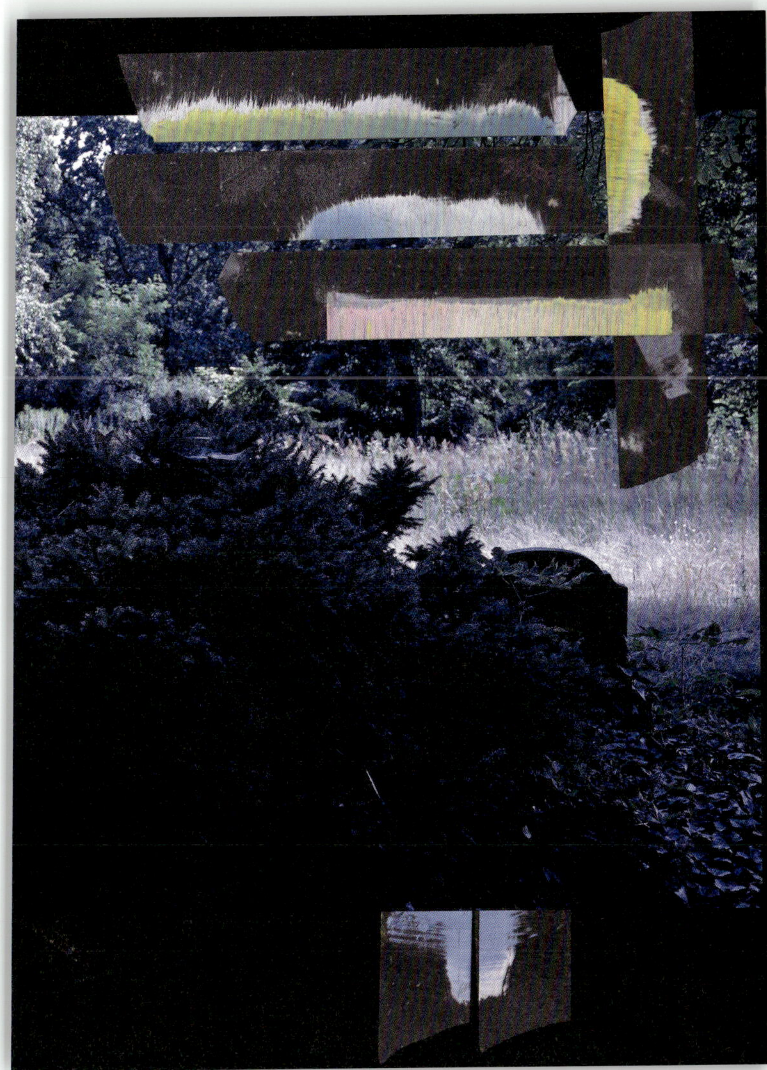

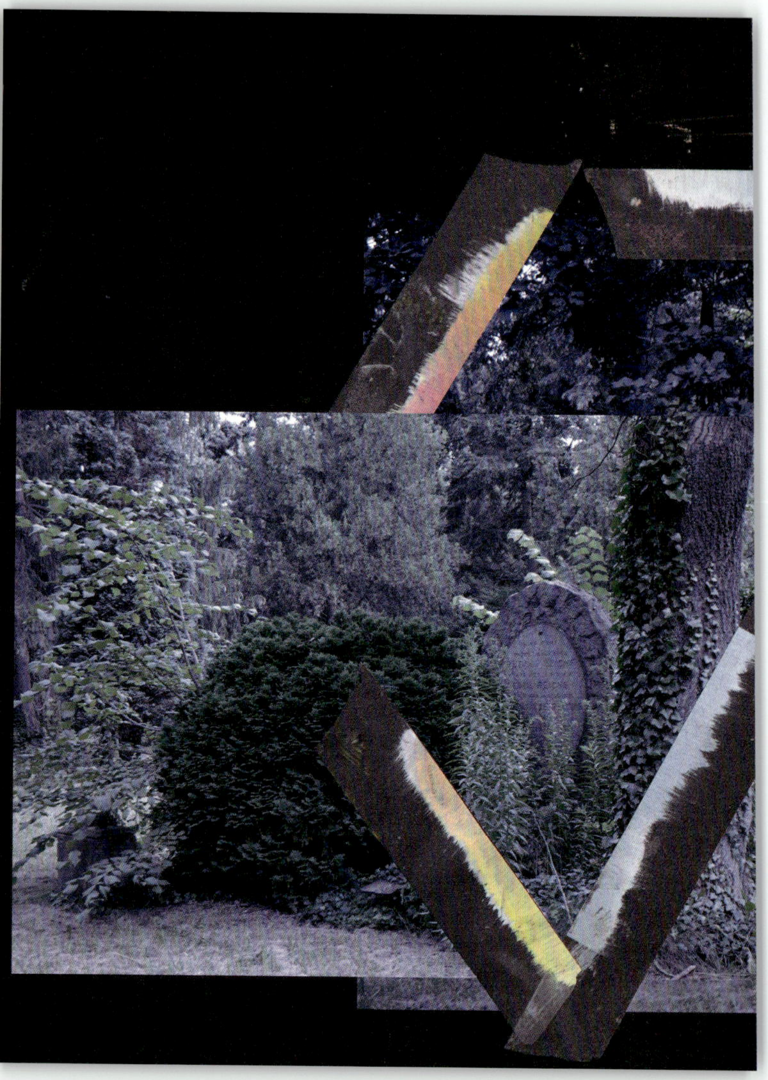

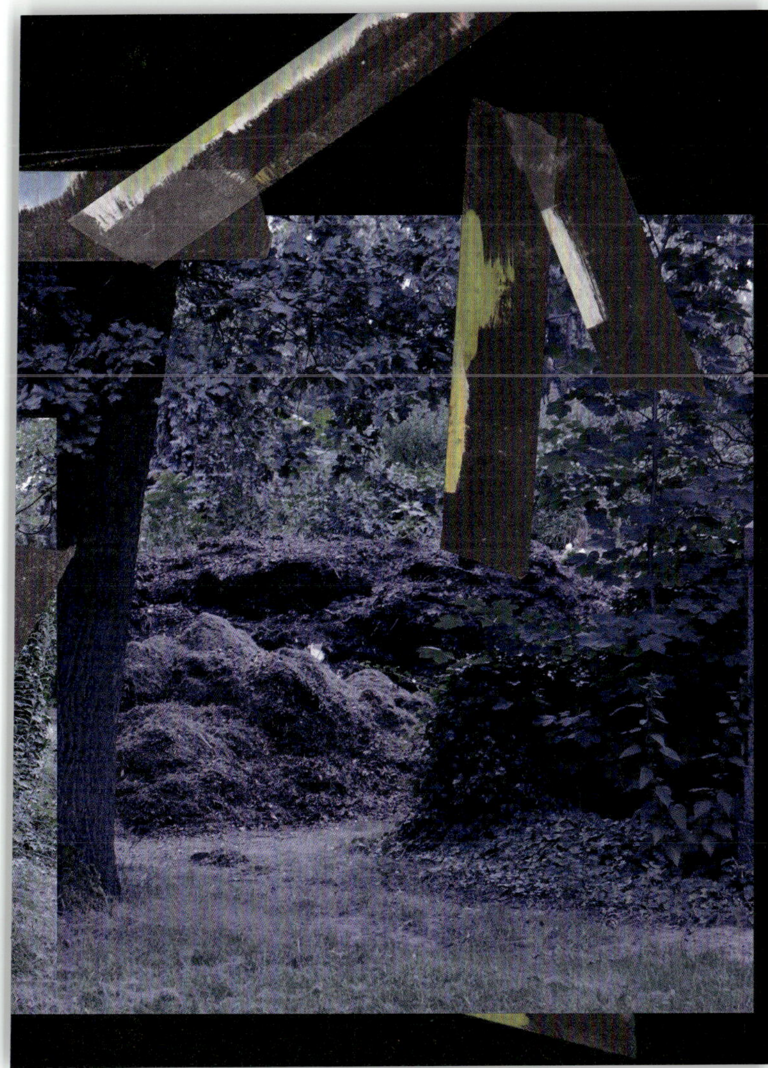

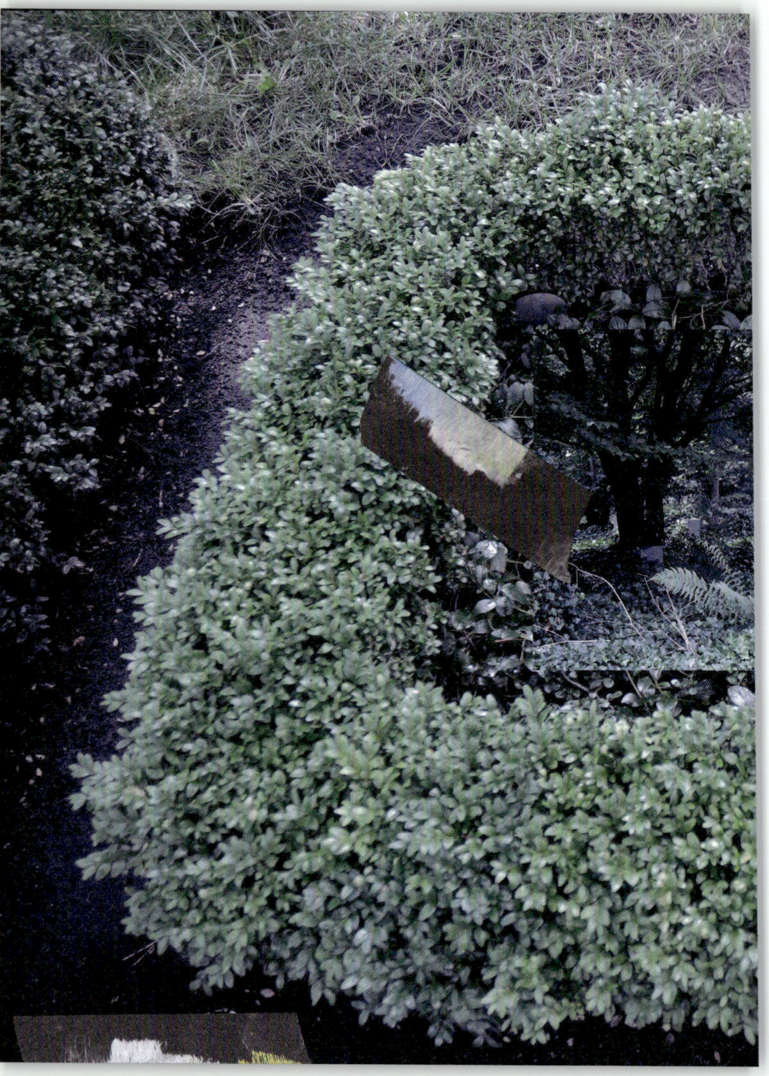

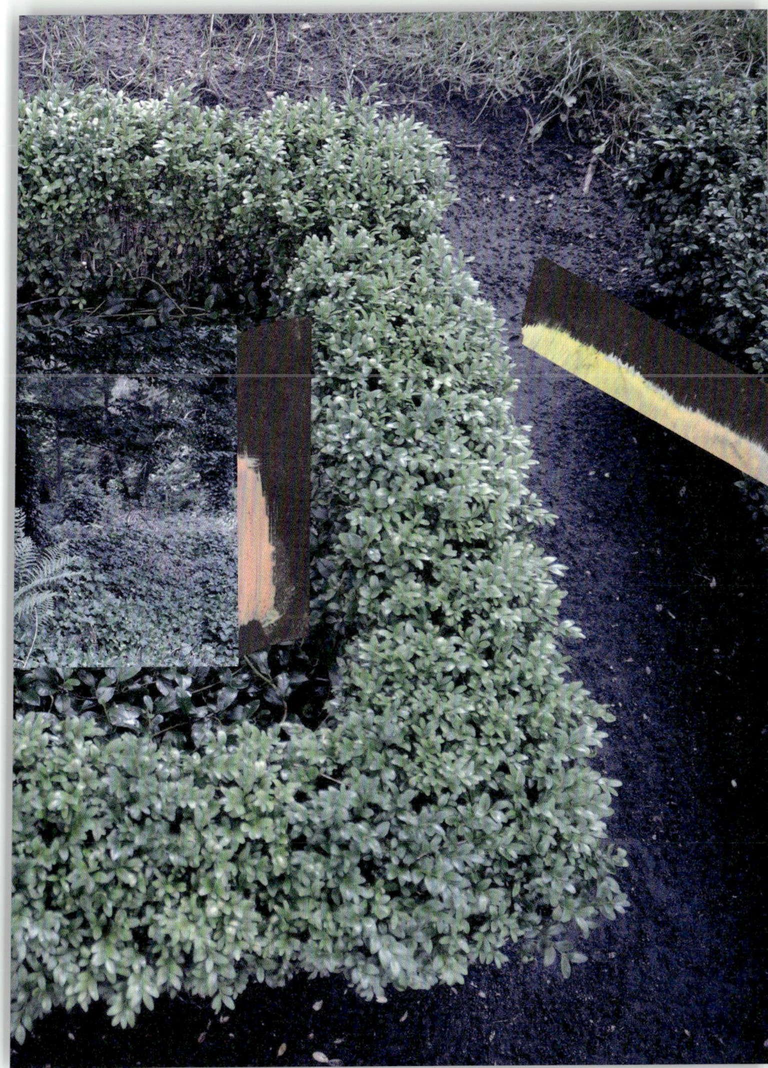

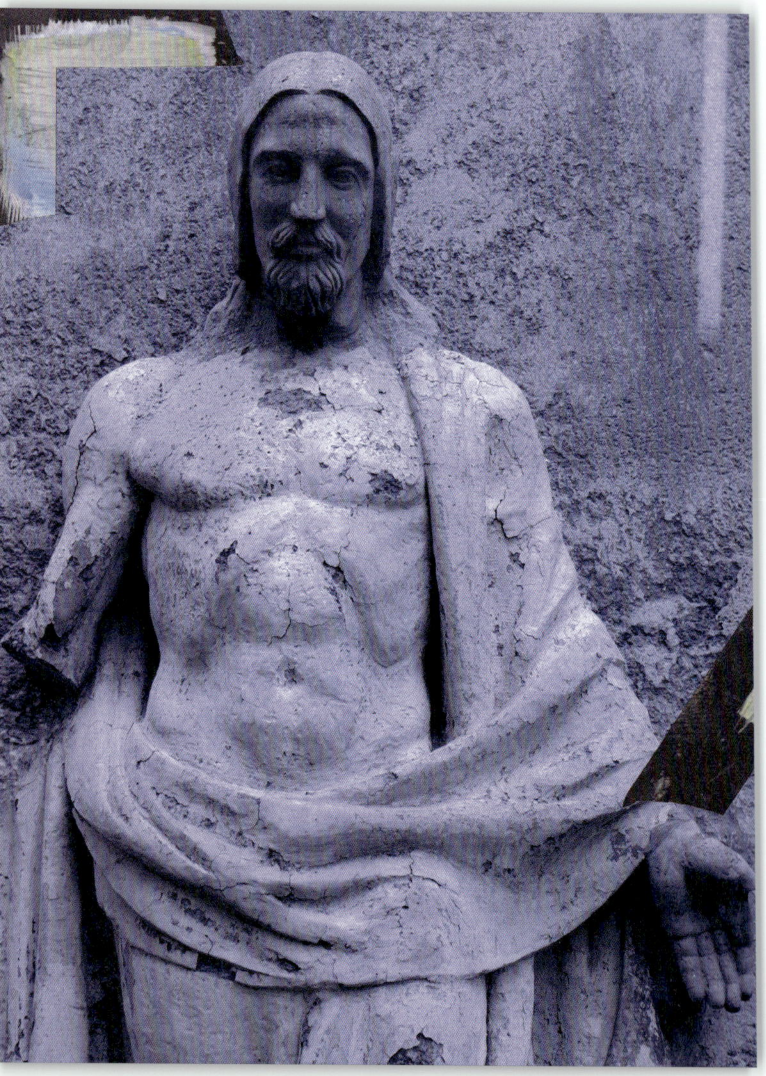

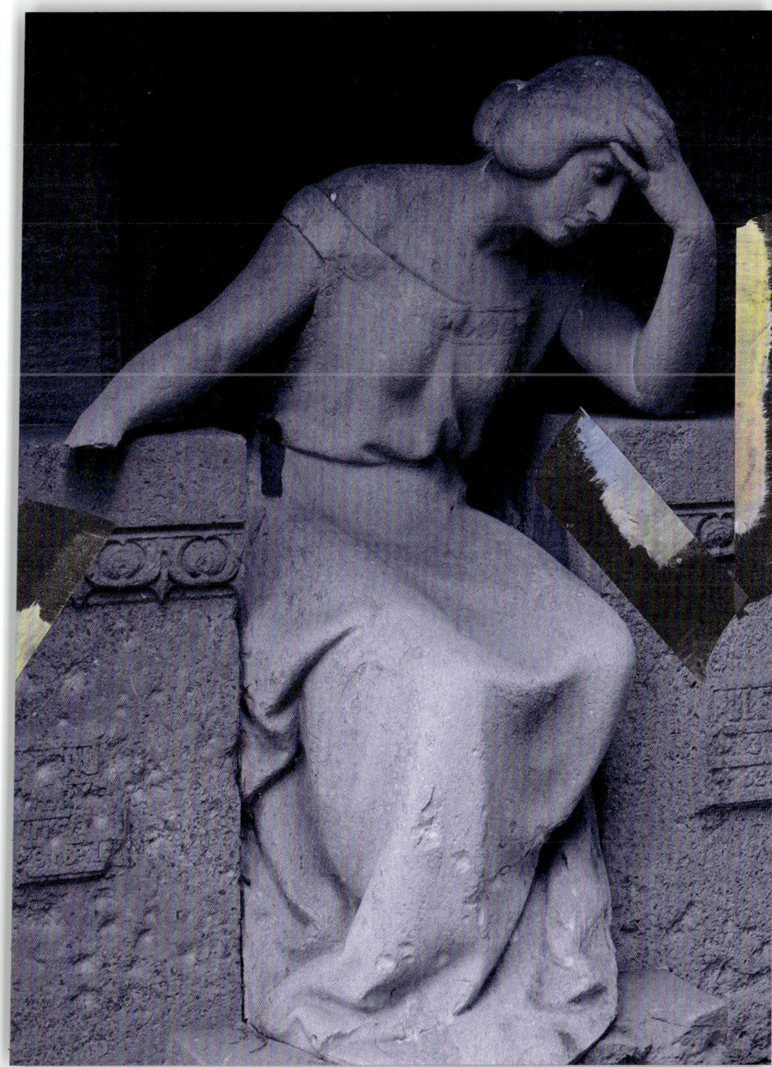

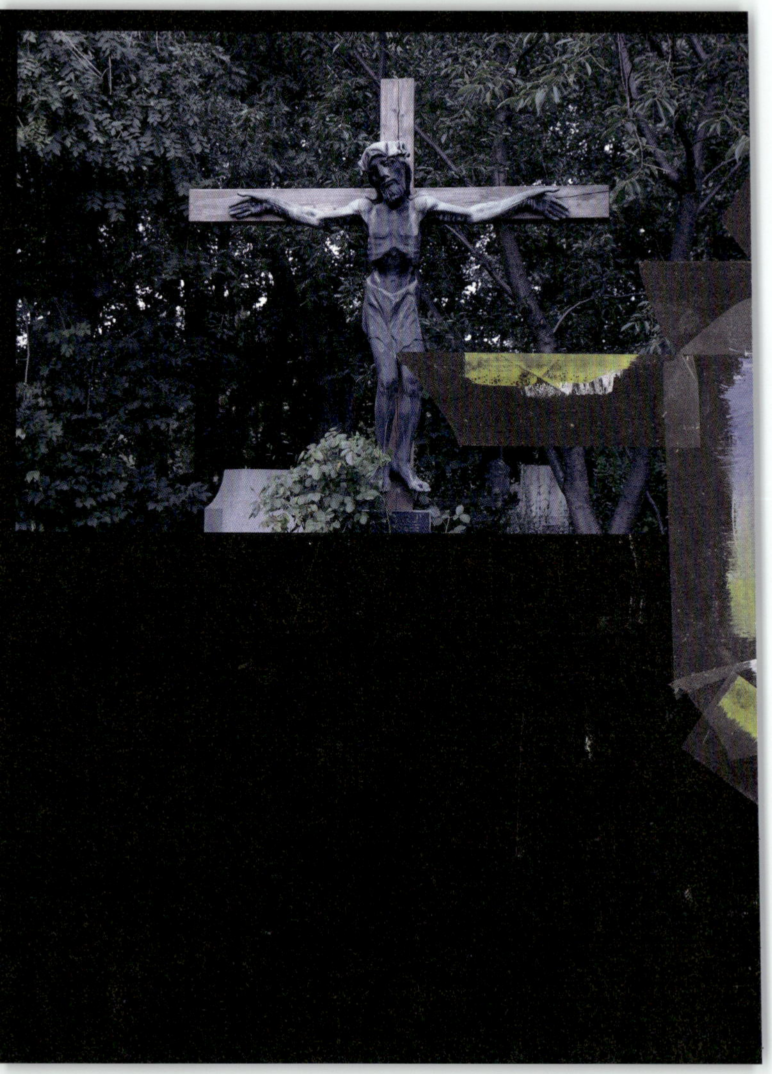

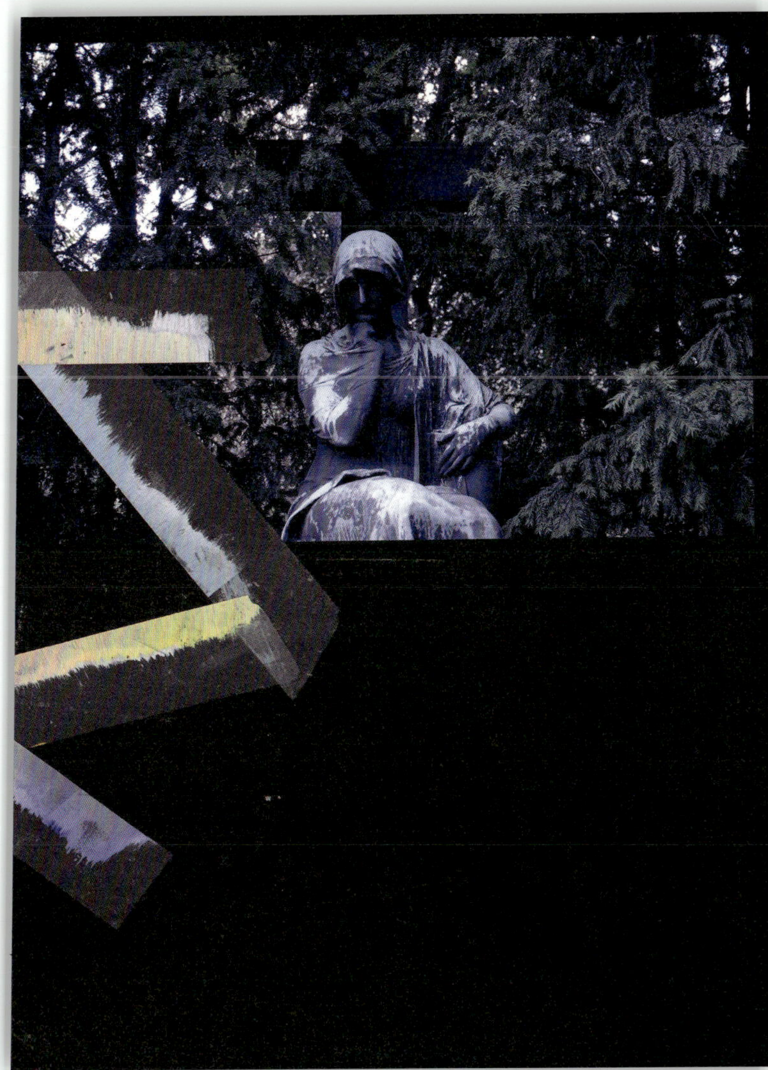

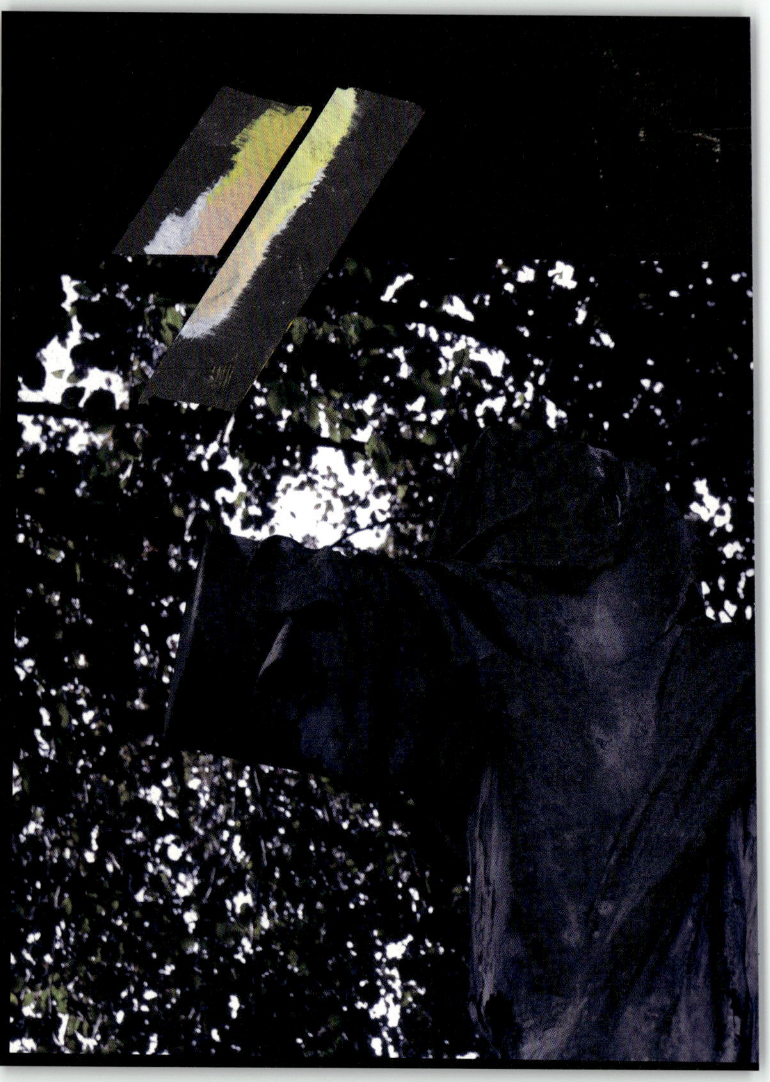

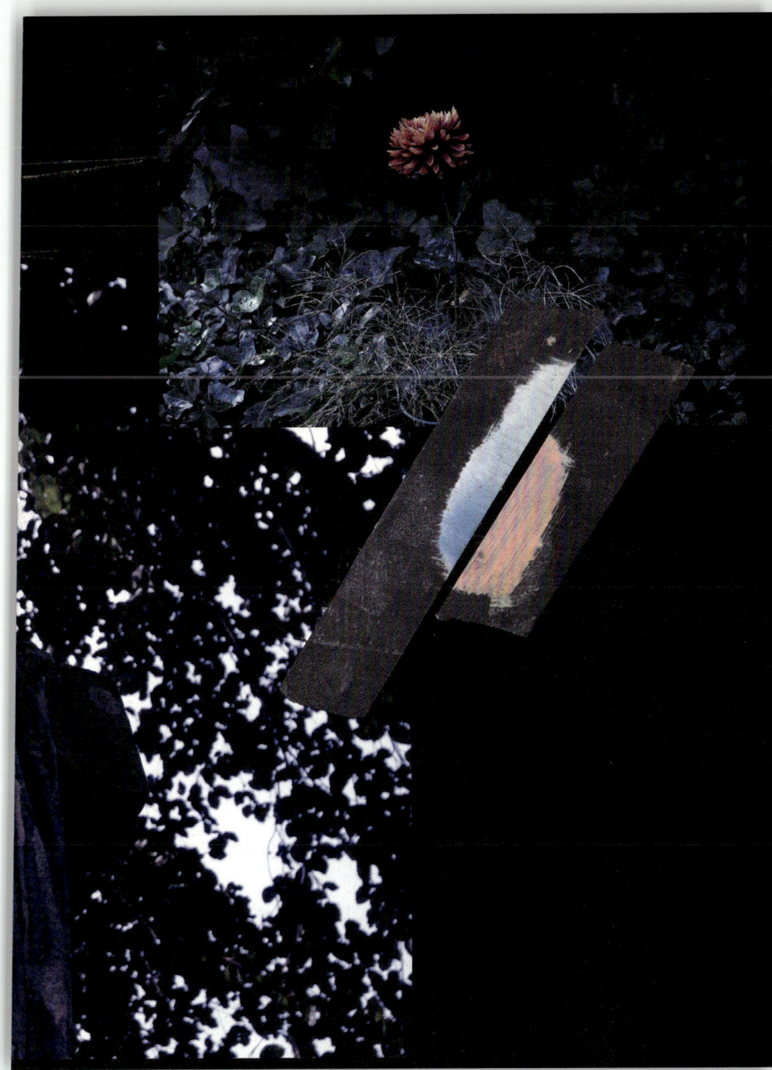

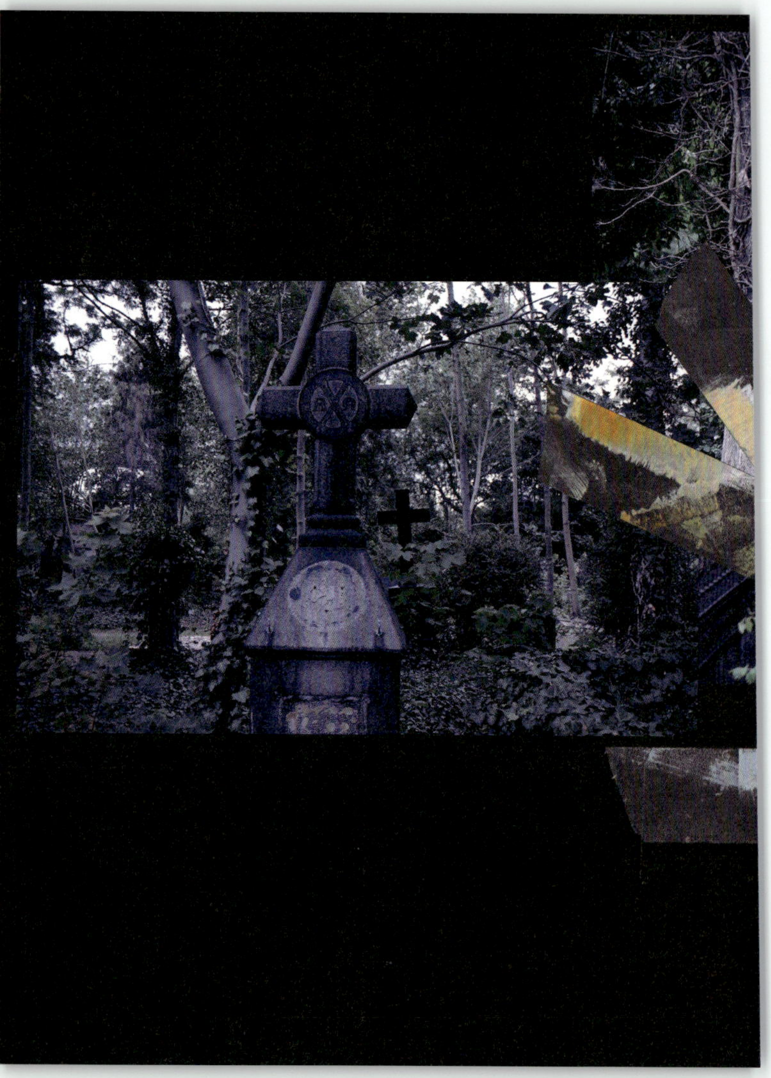

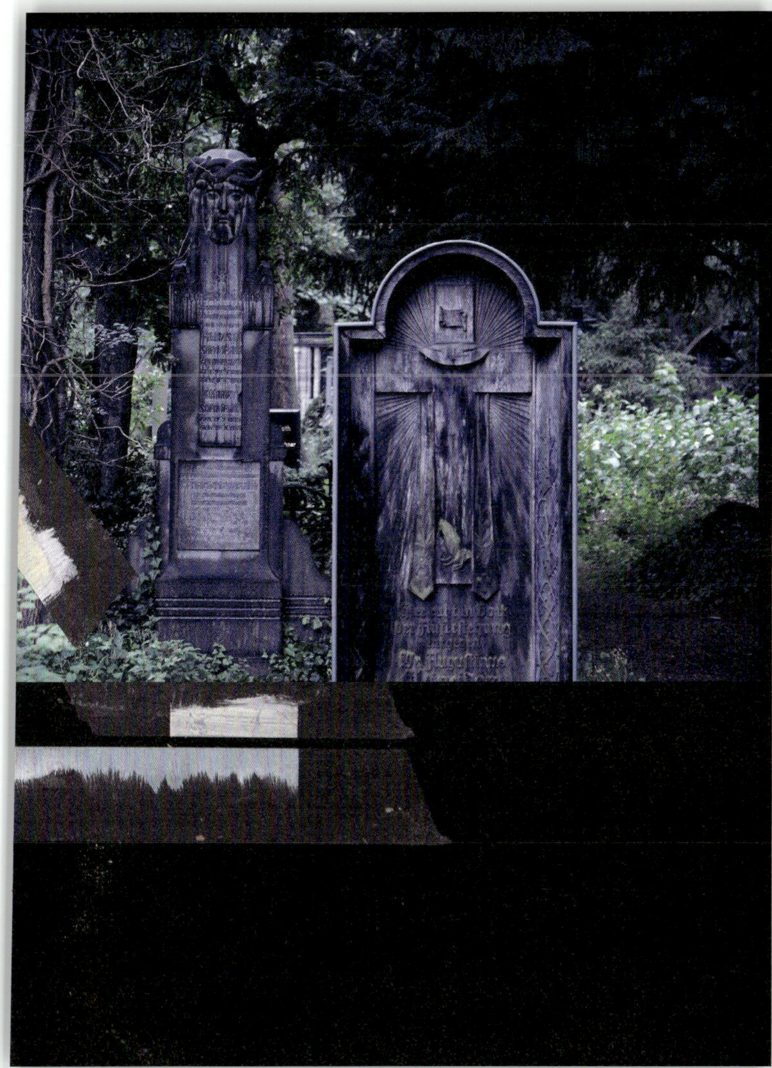

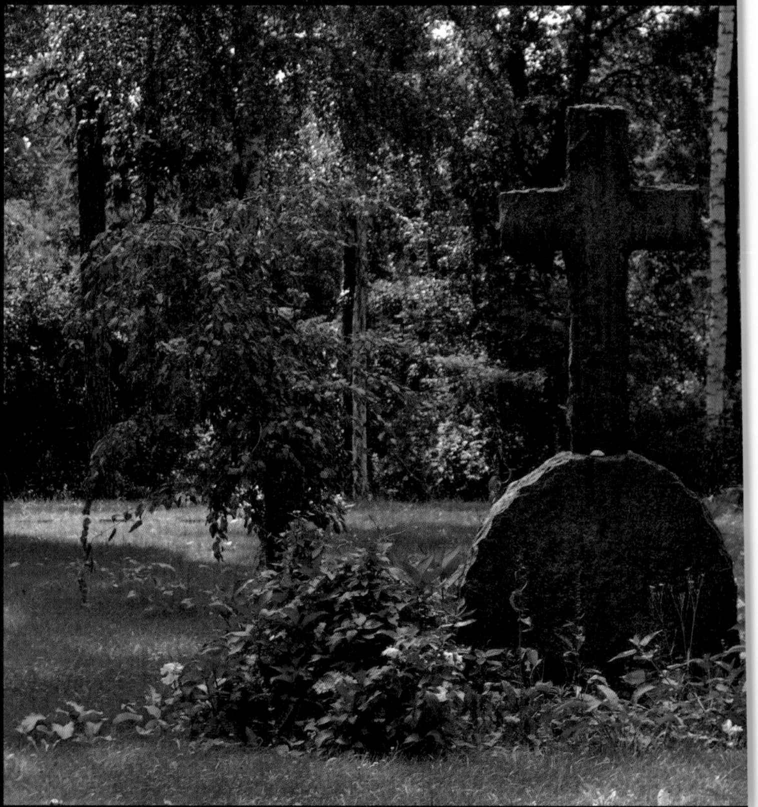

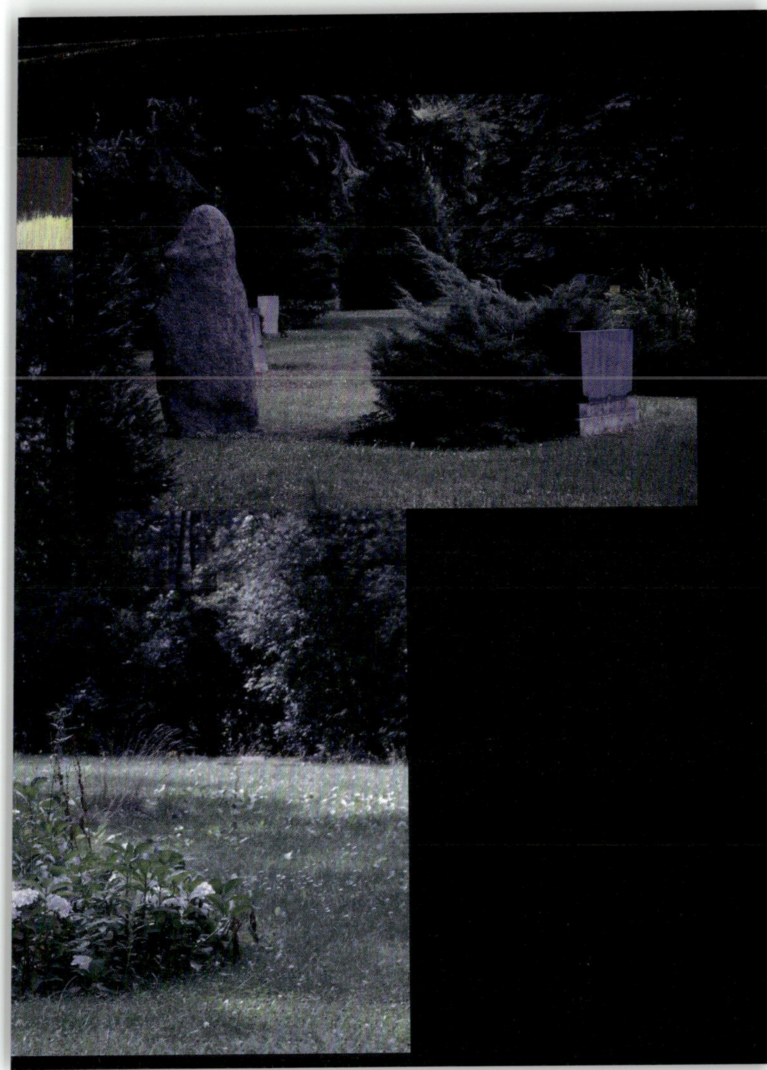

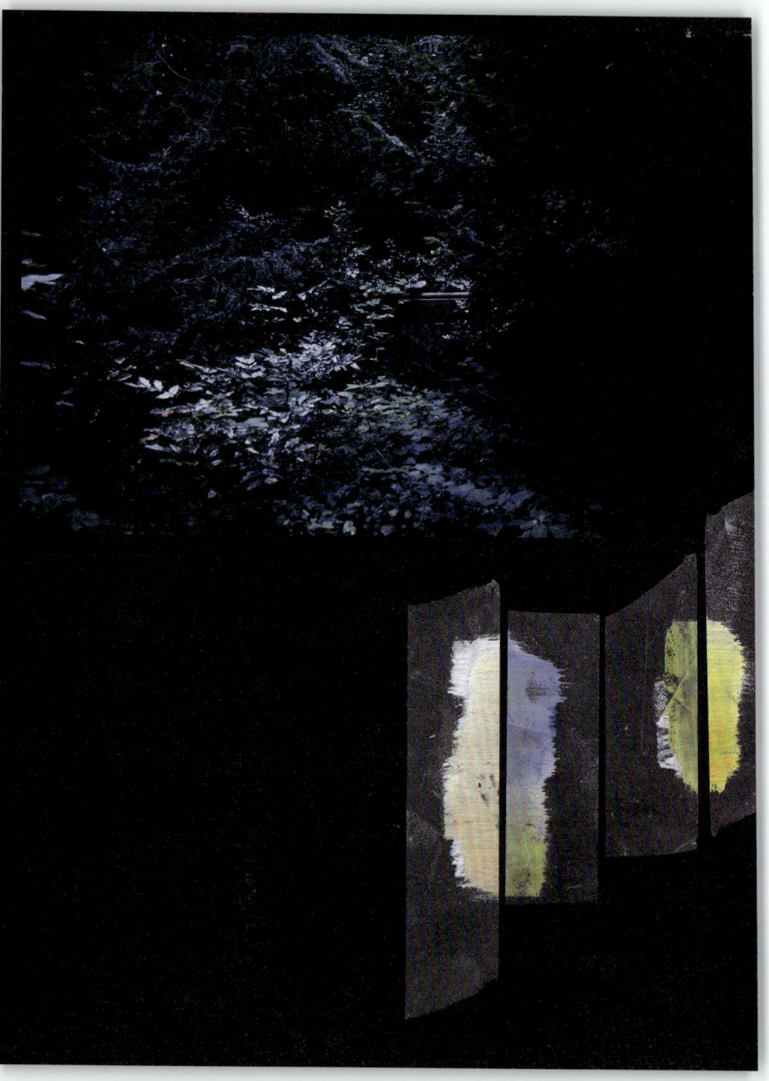

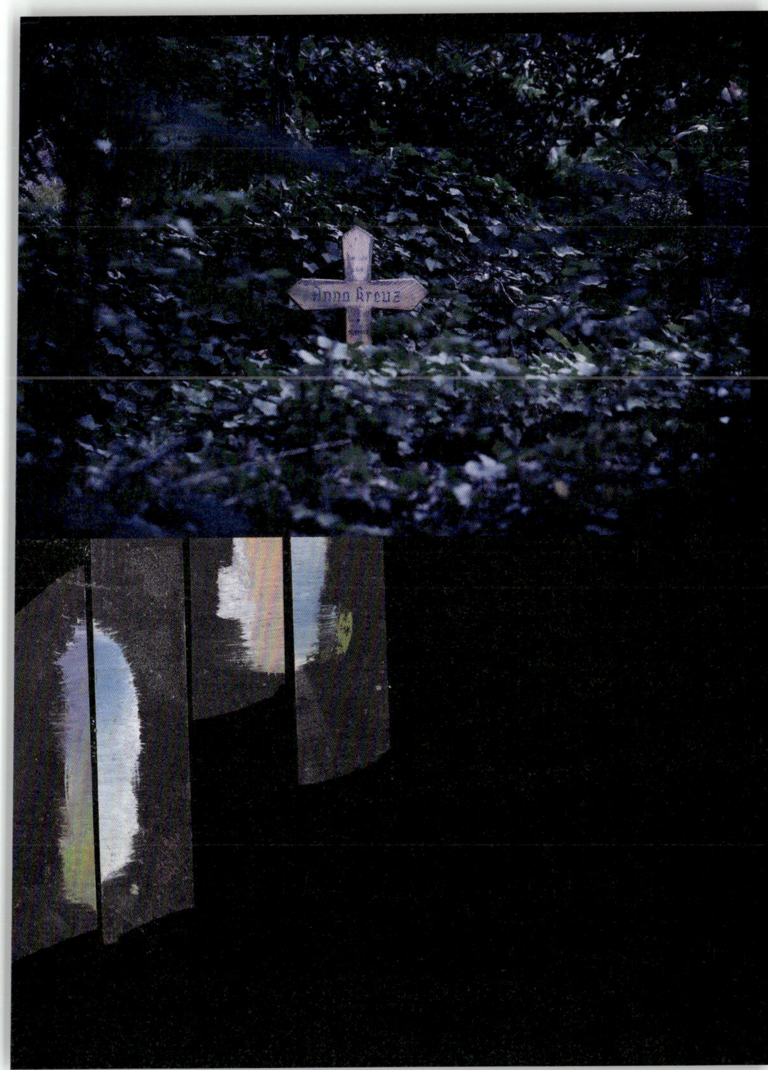
Anna Kreuz

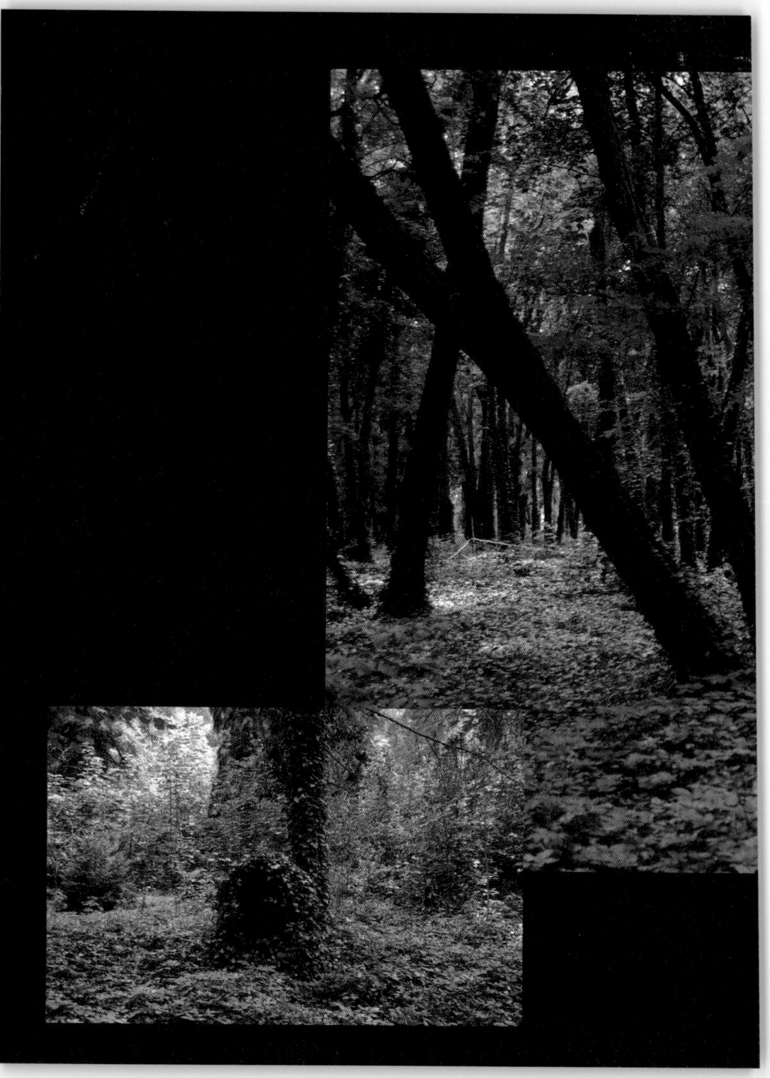

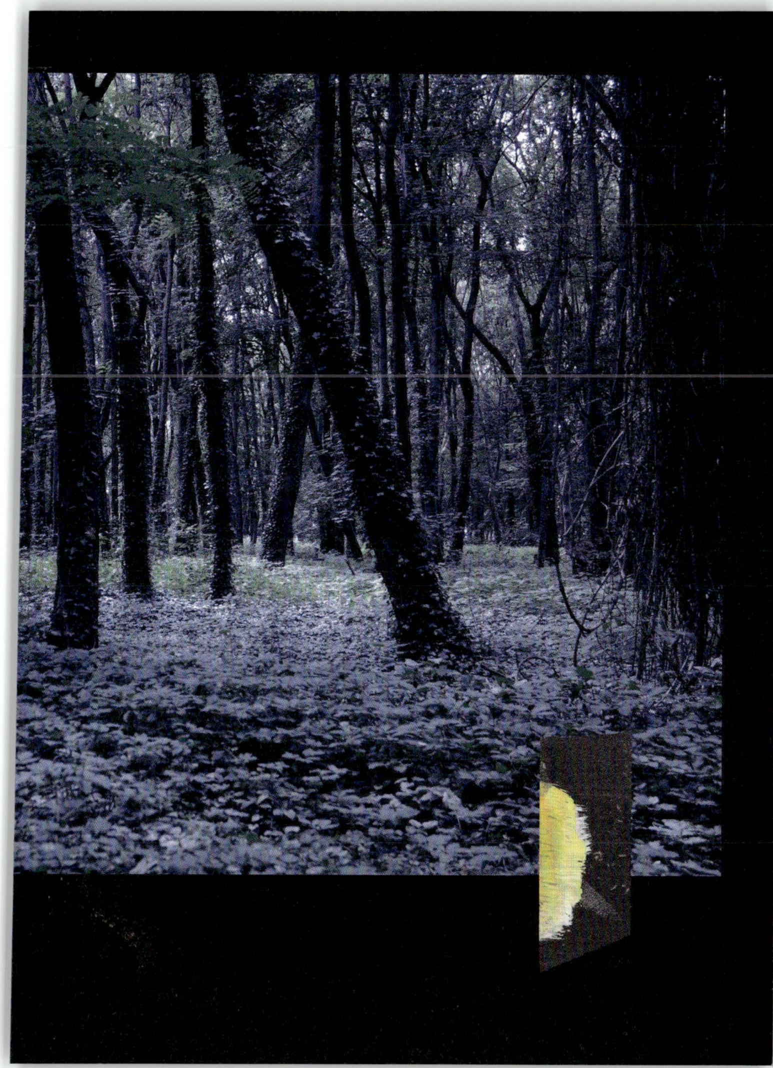

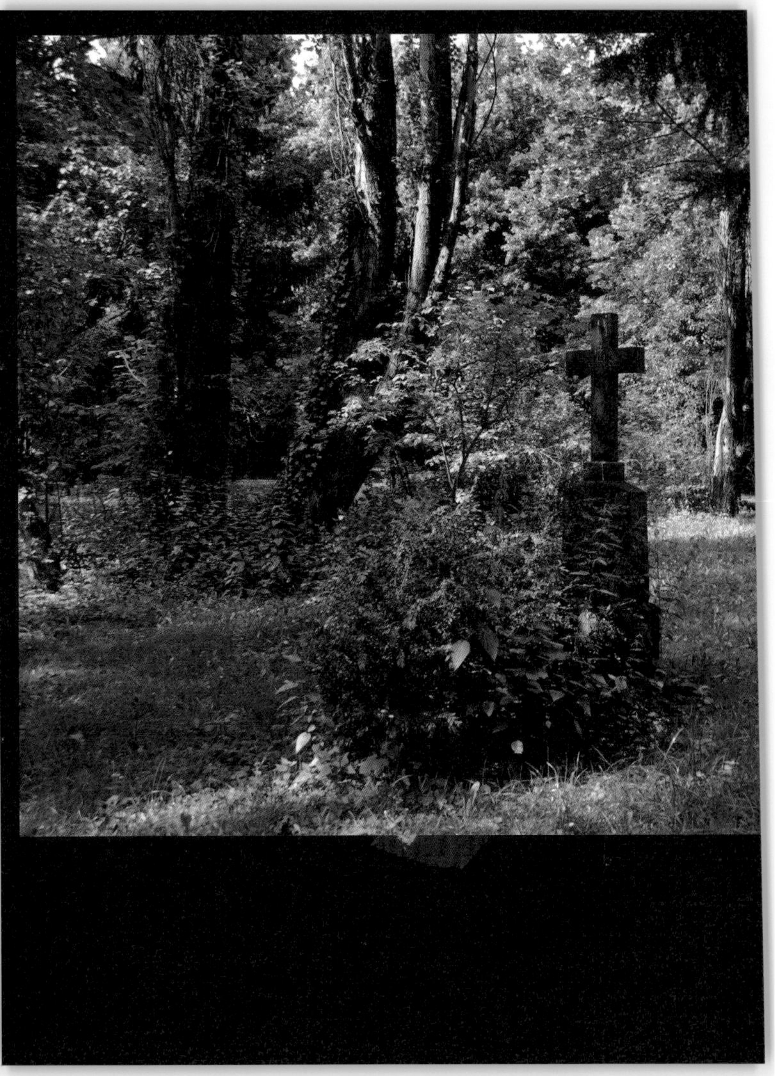

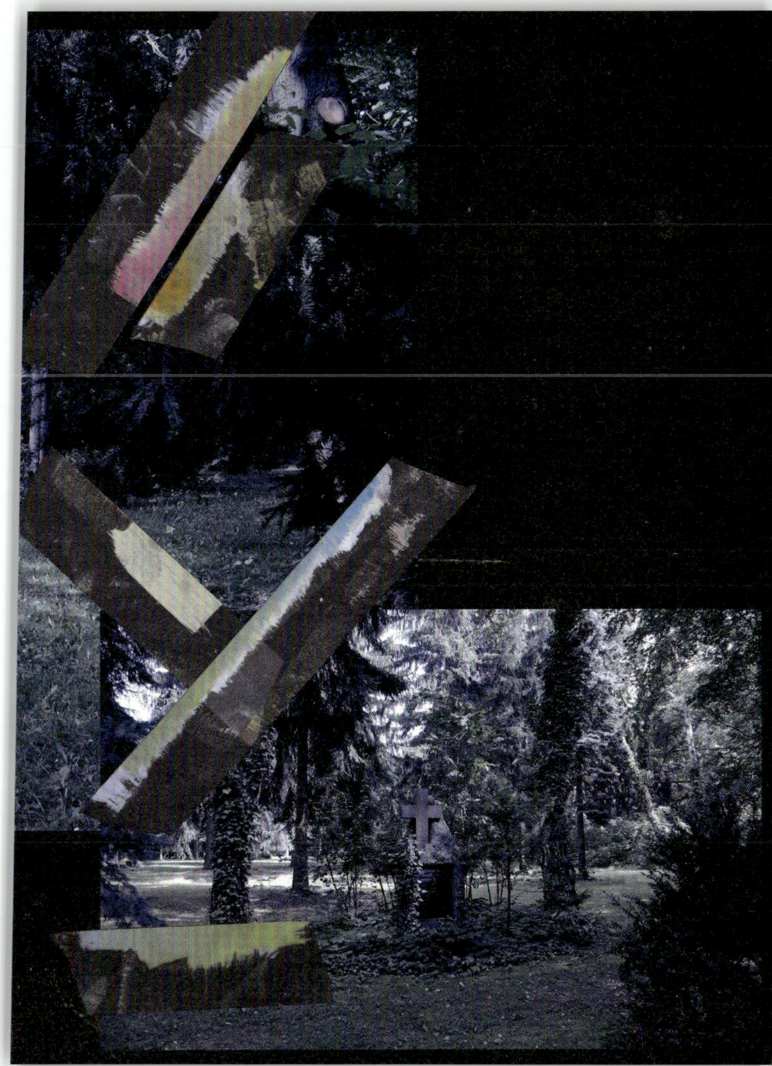

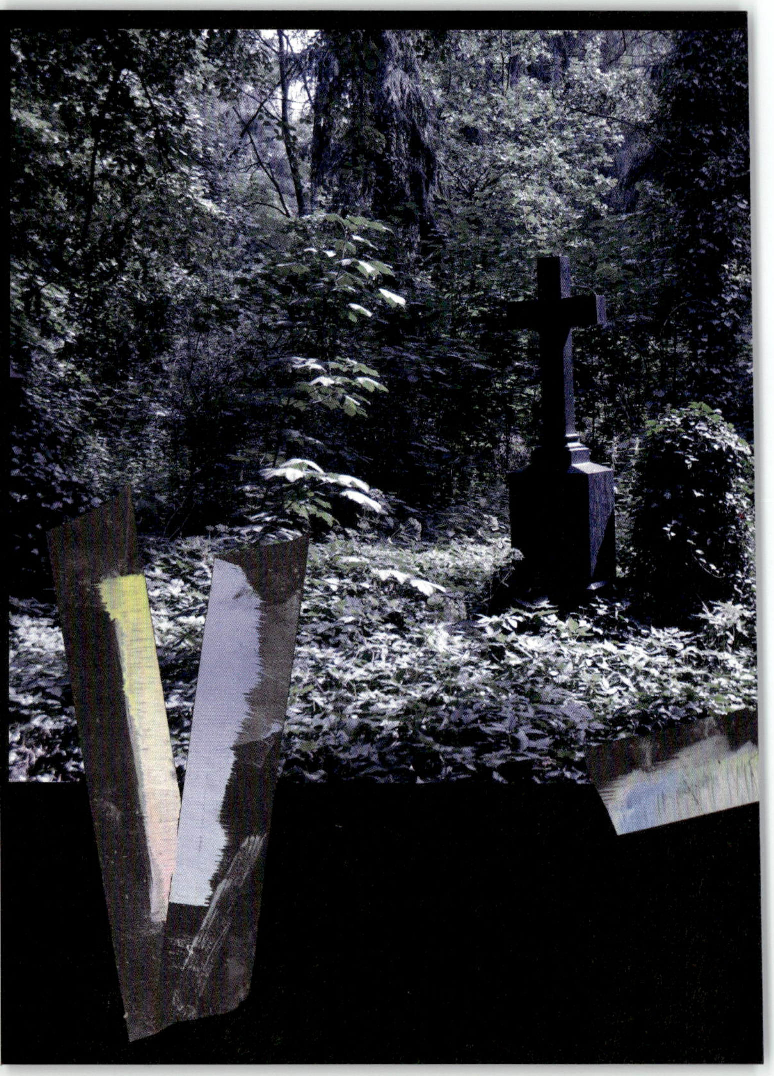

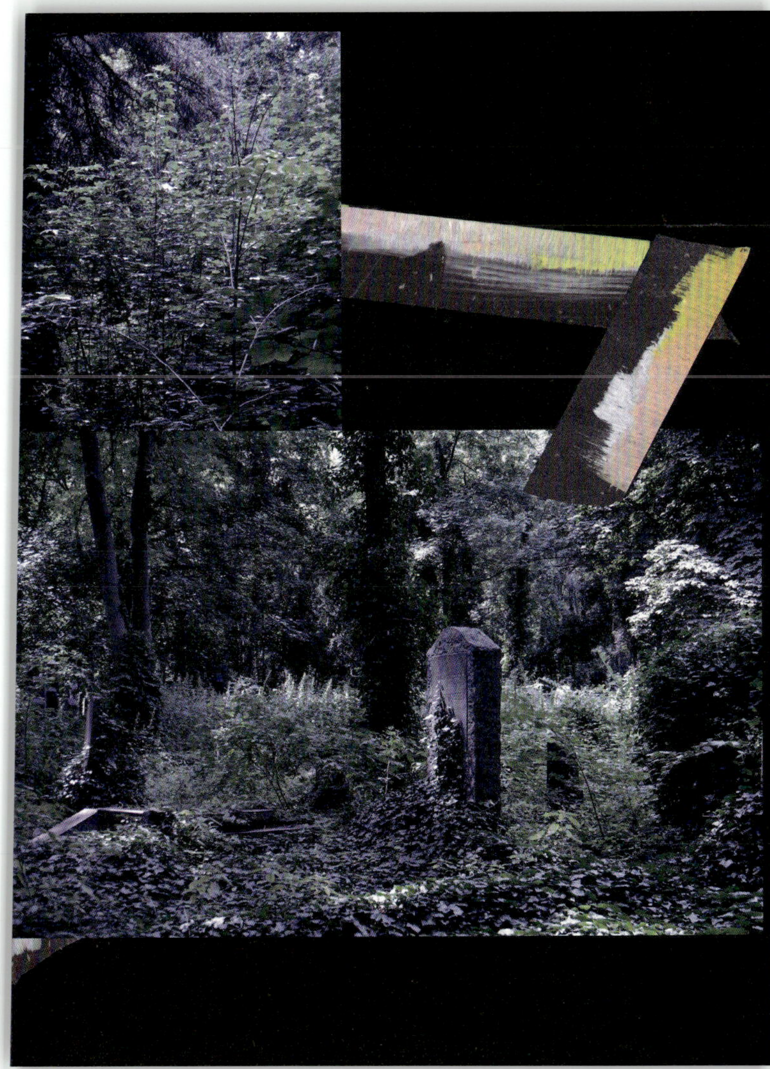

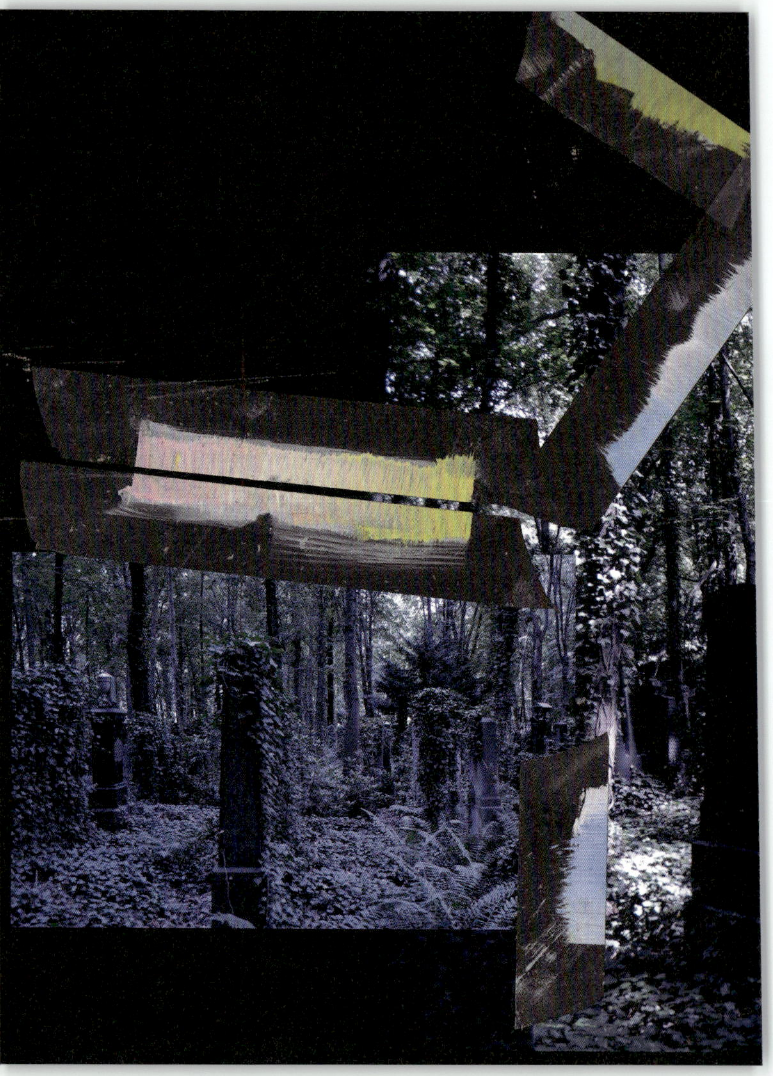

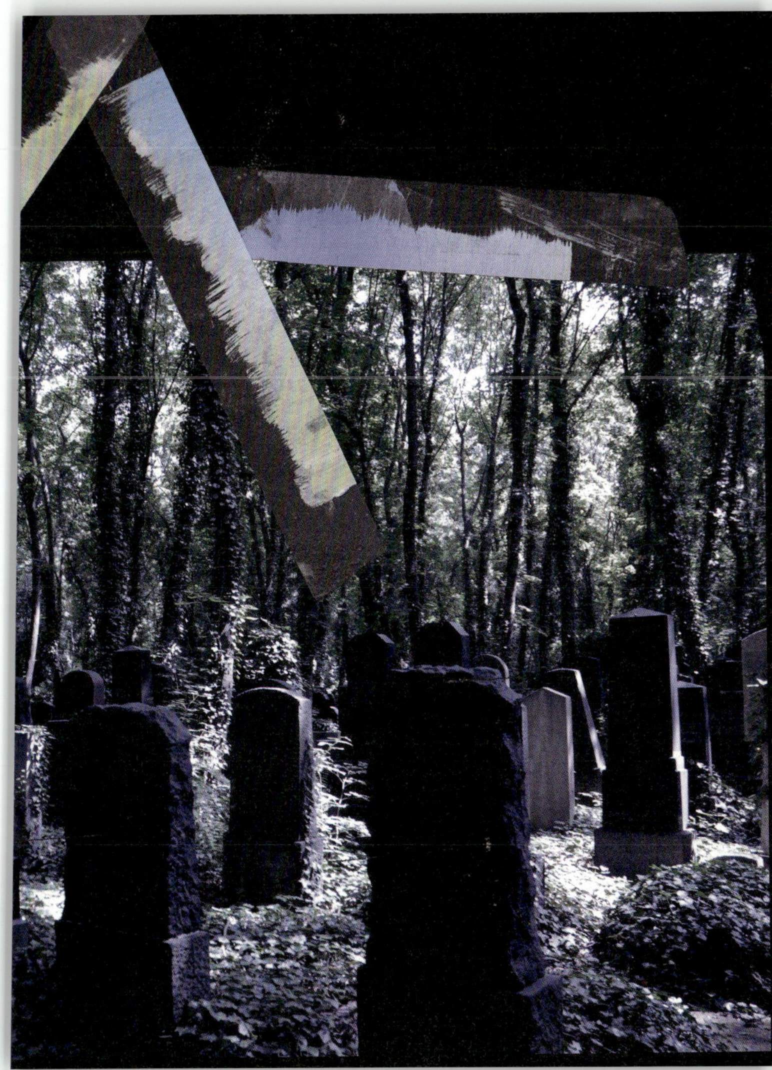

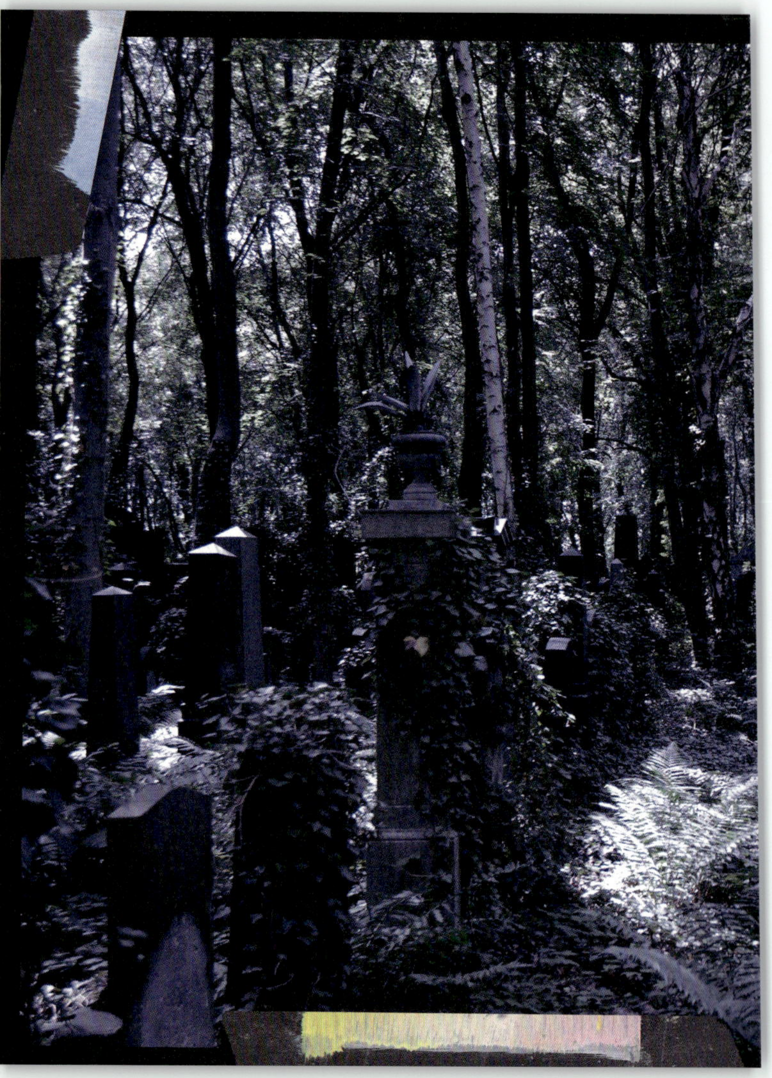

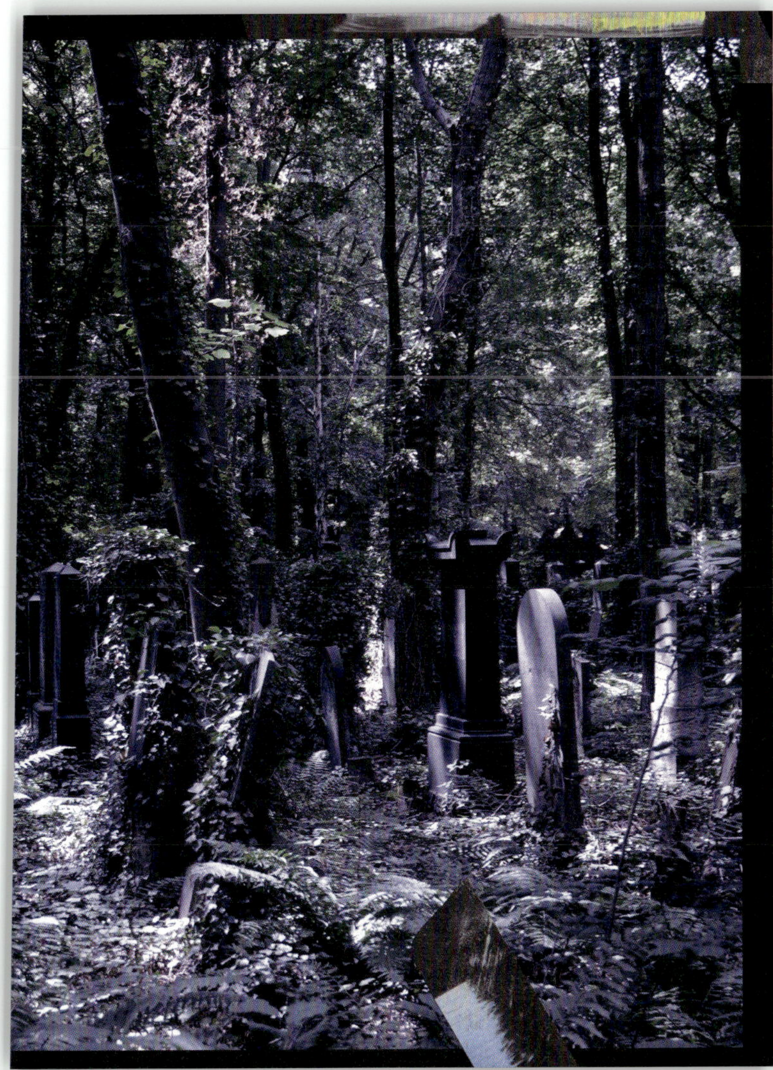

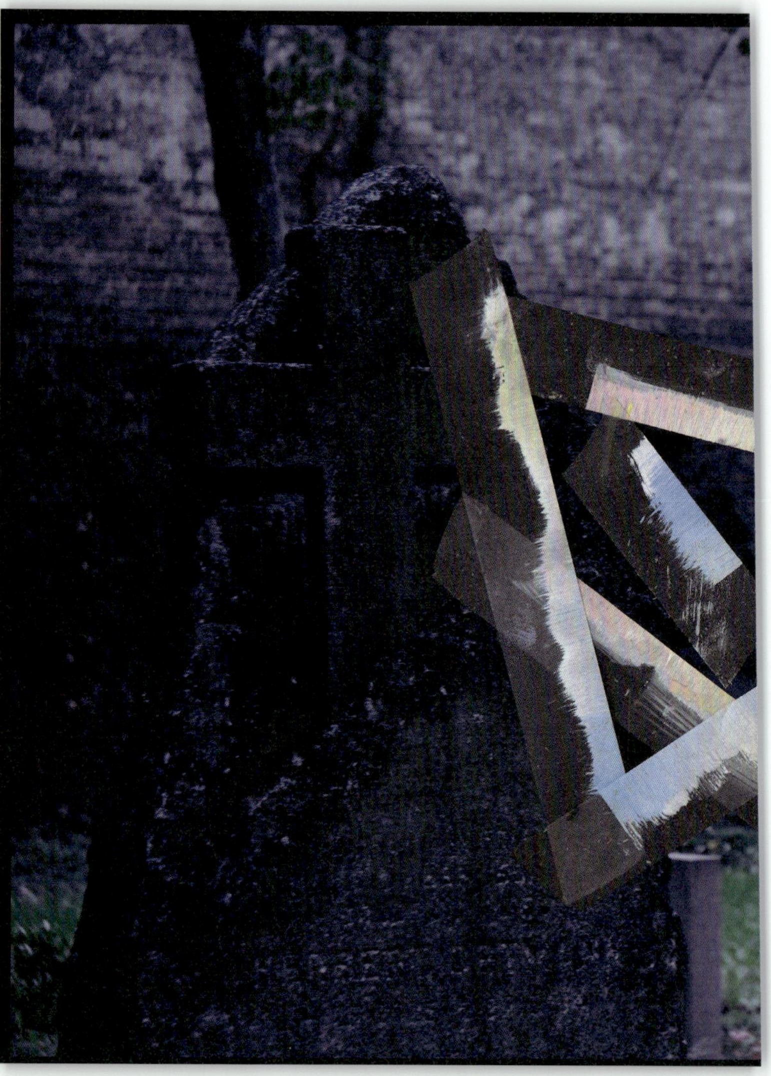

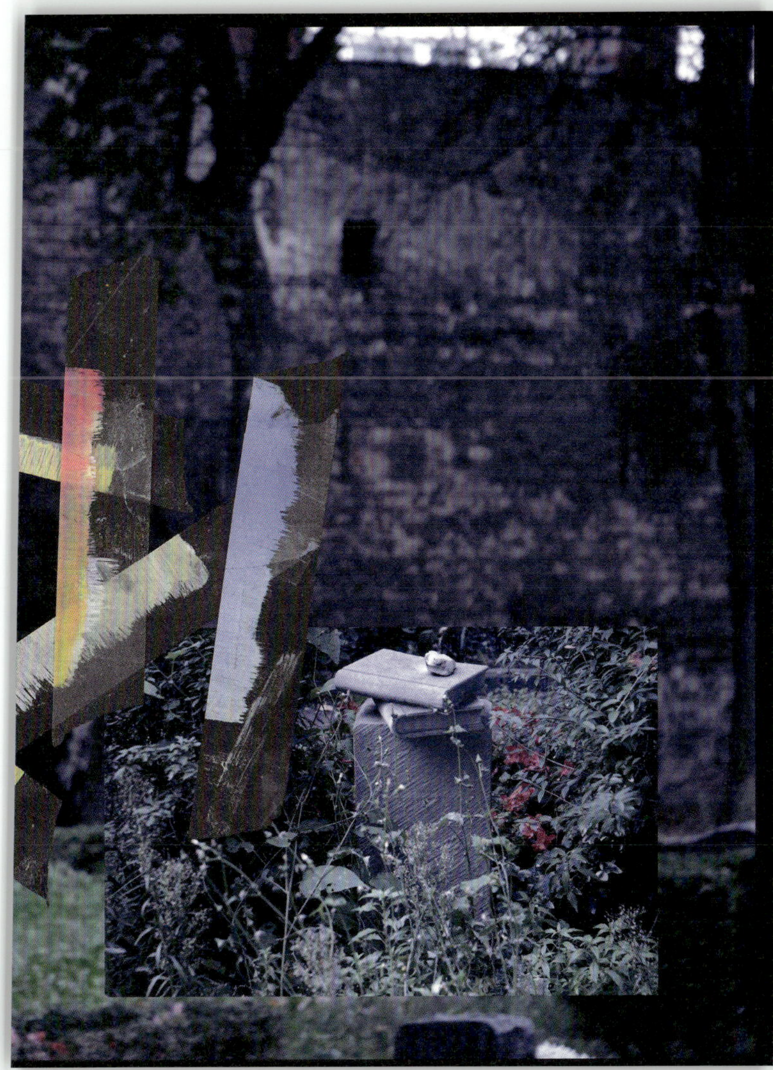

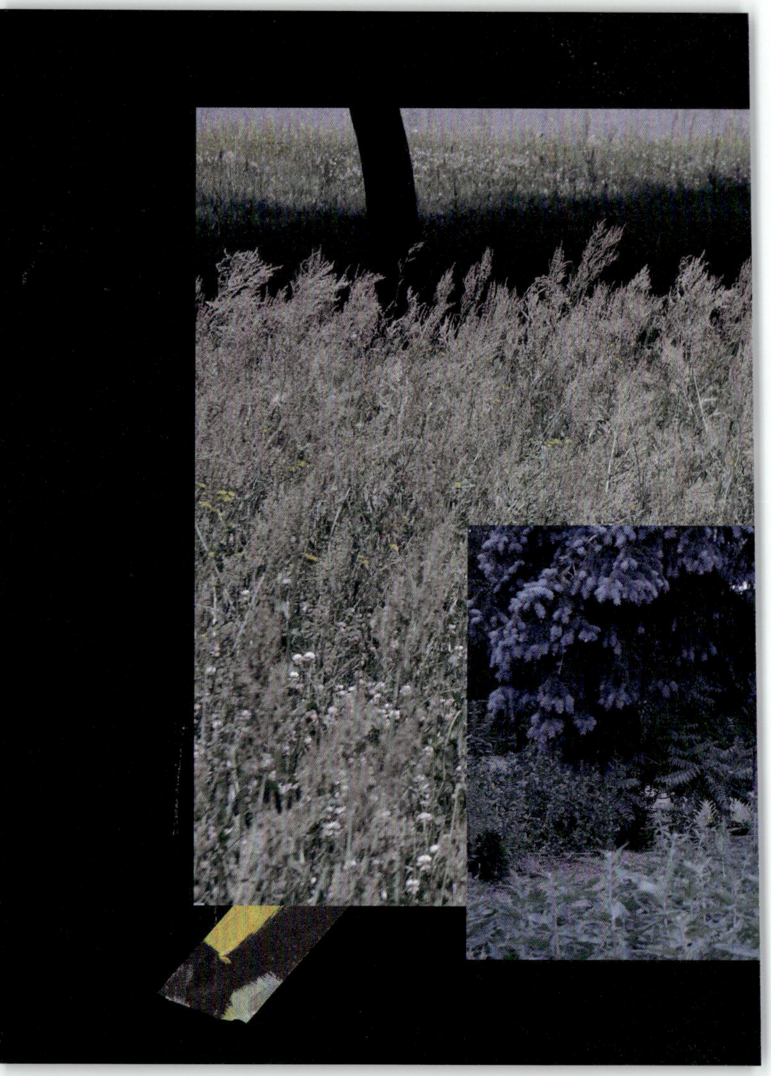

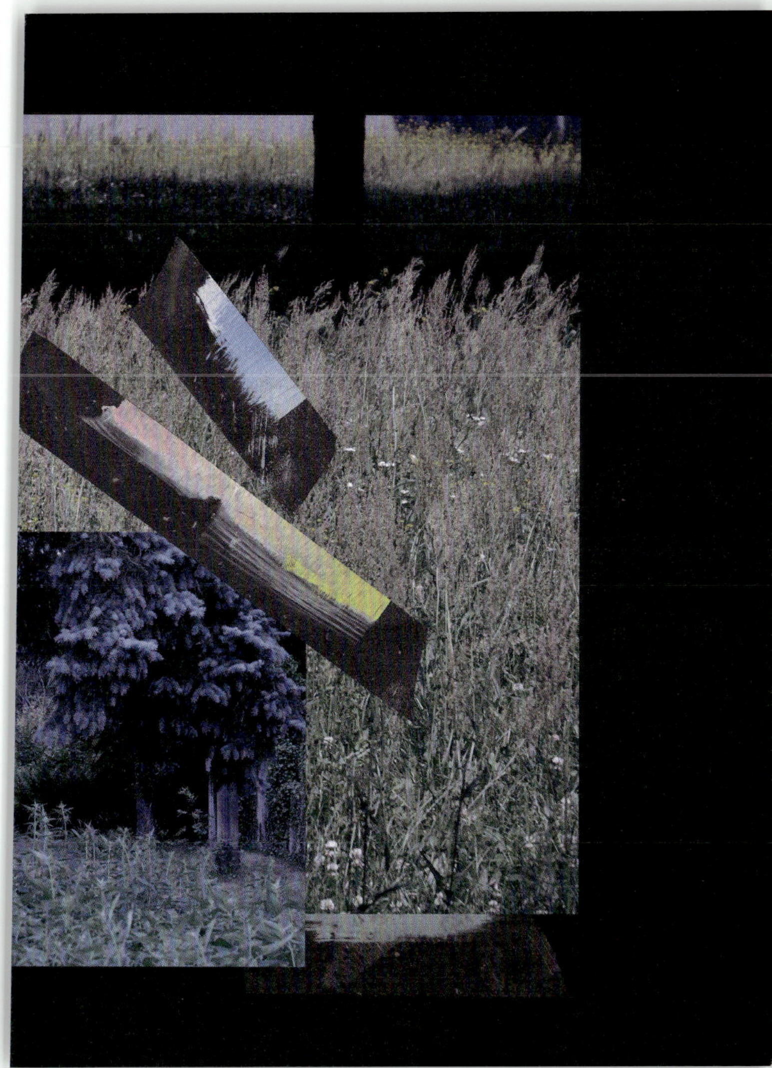

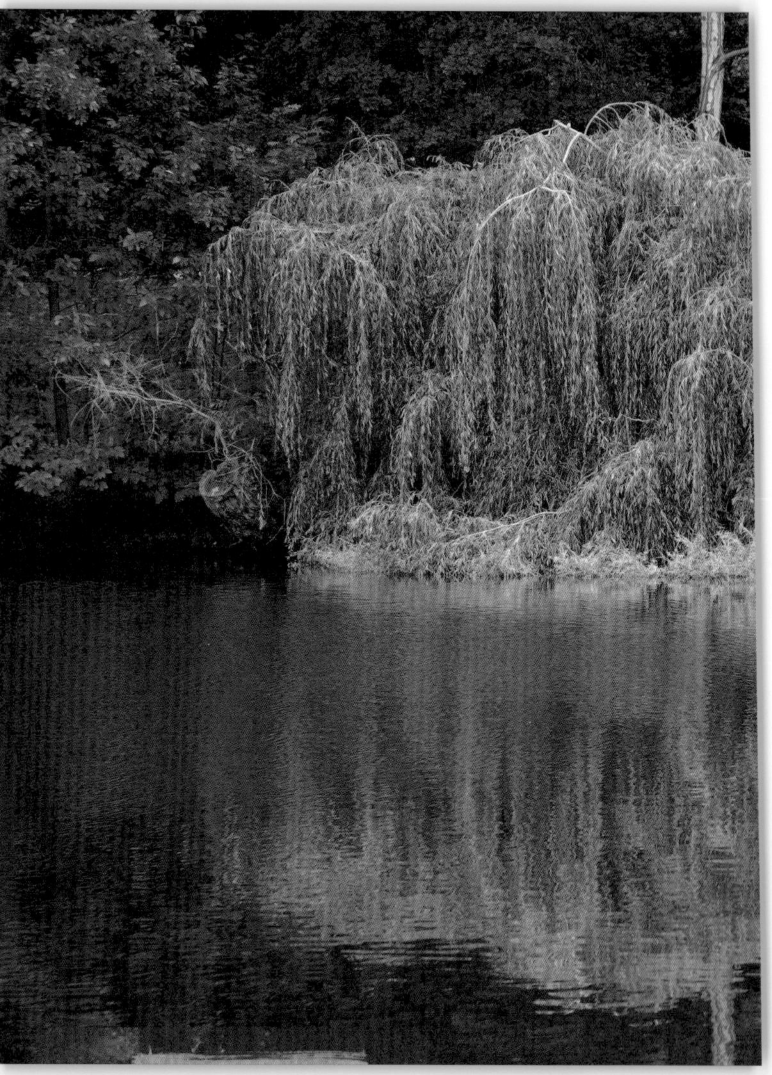

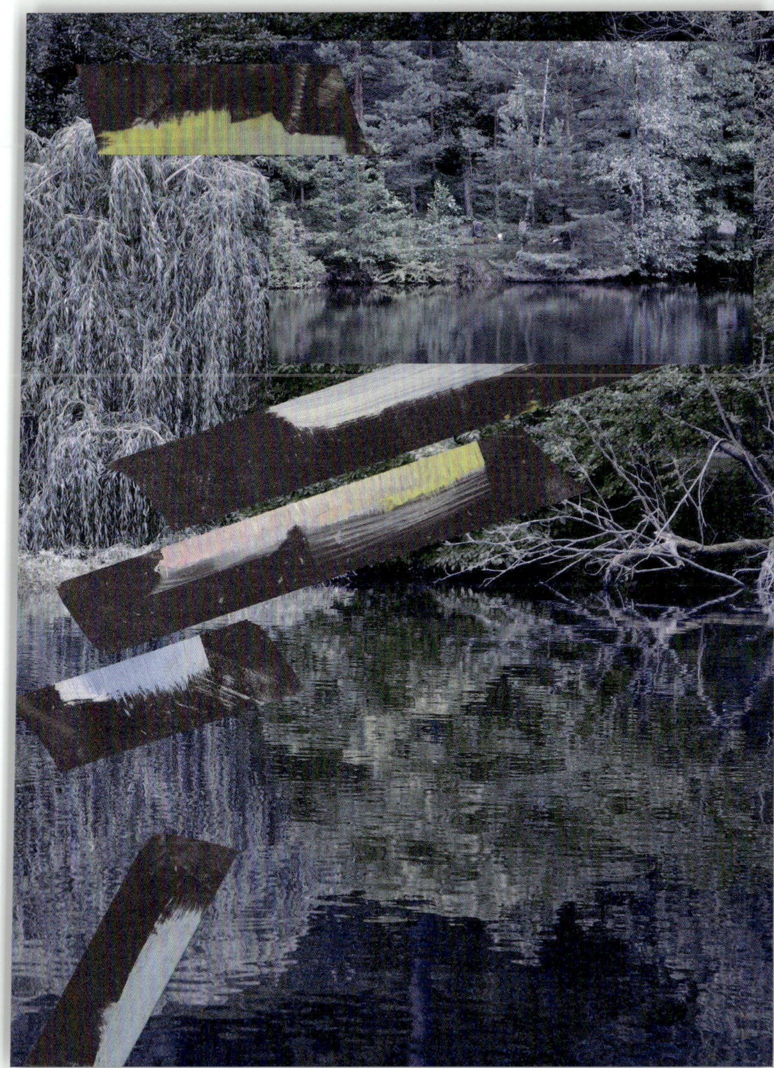

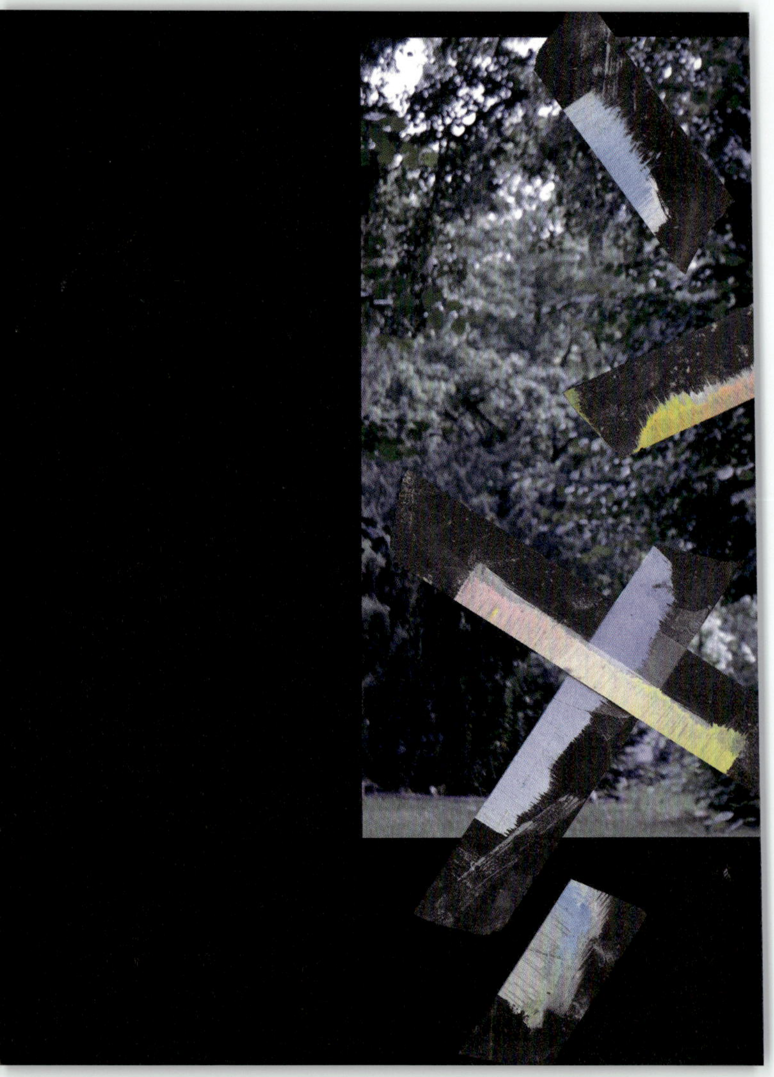

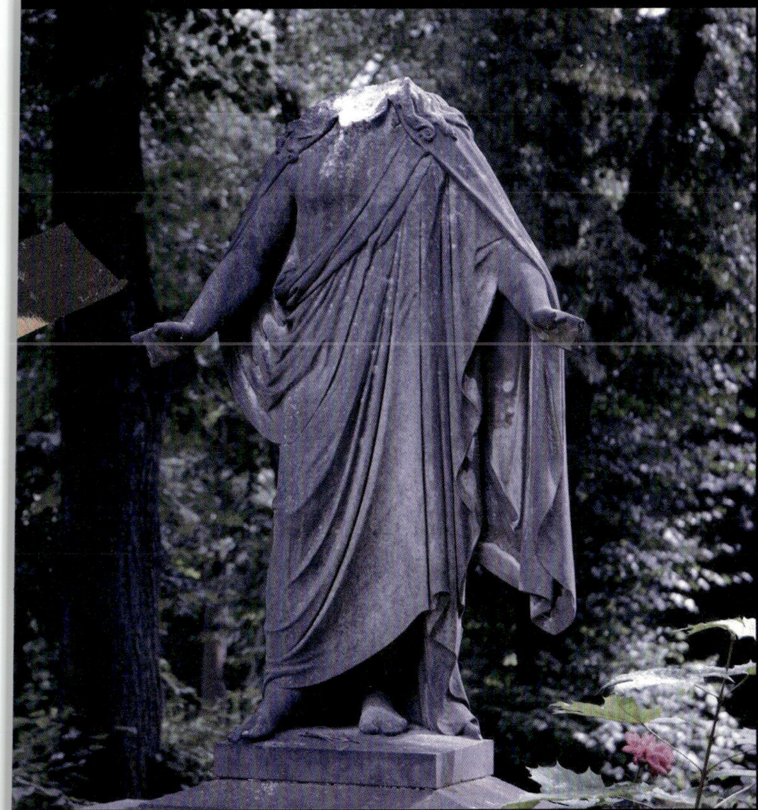

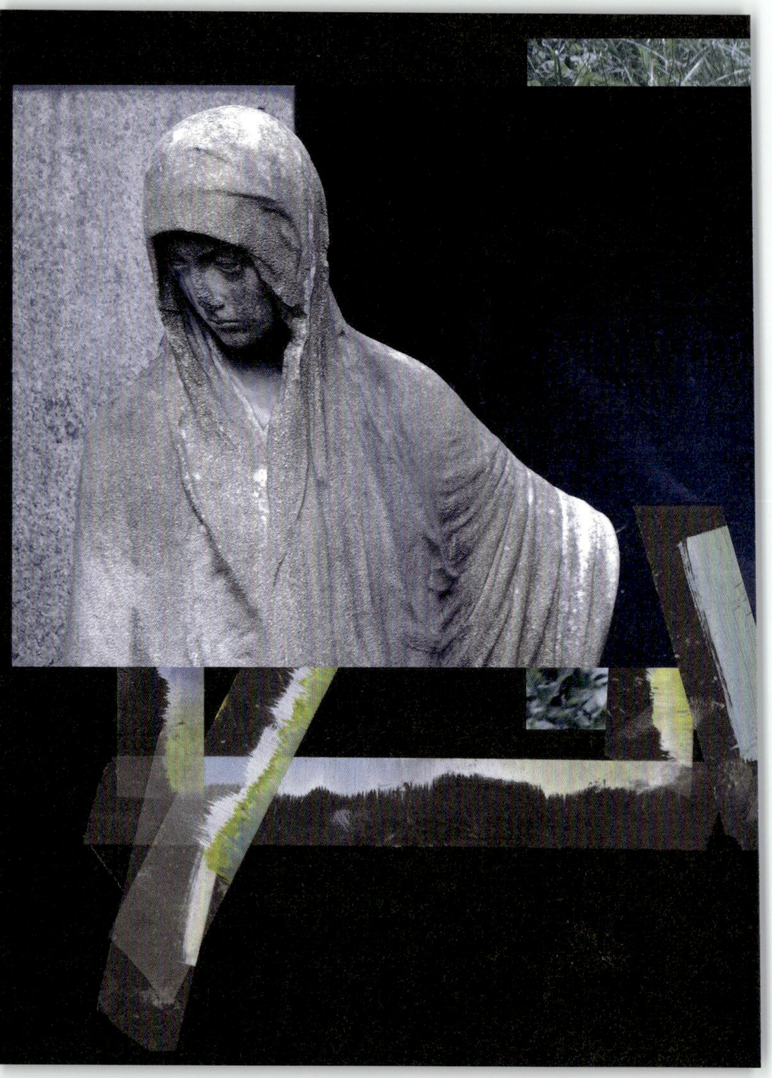

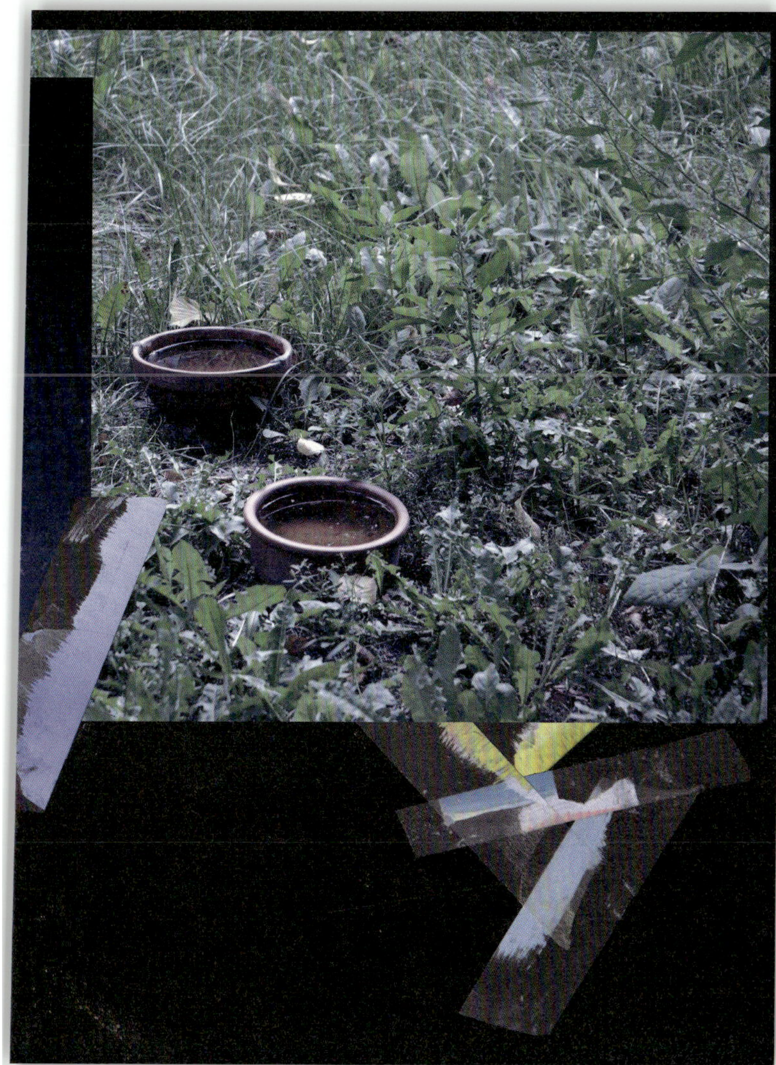

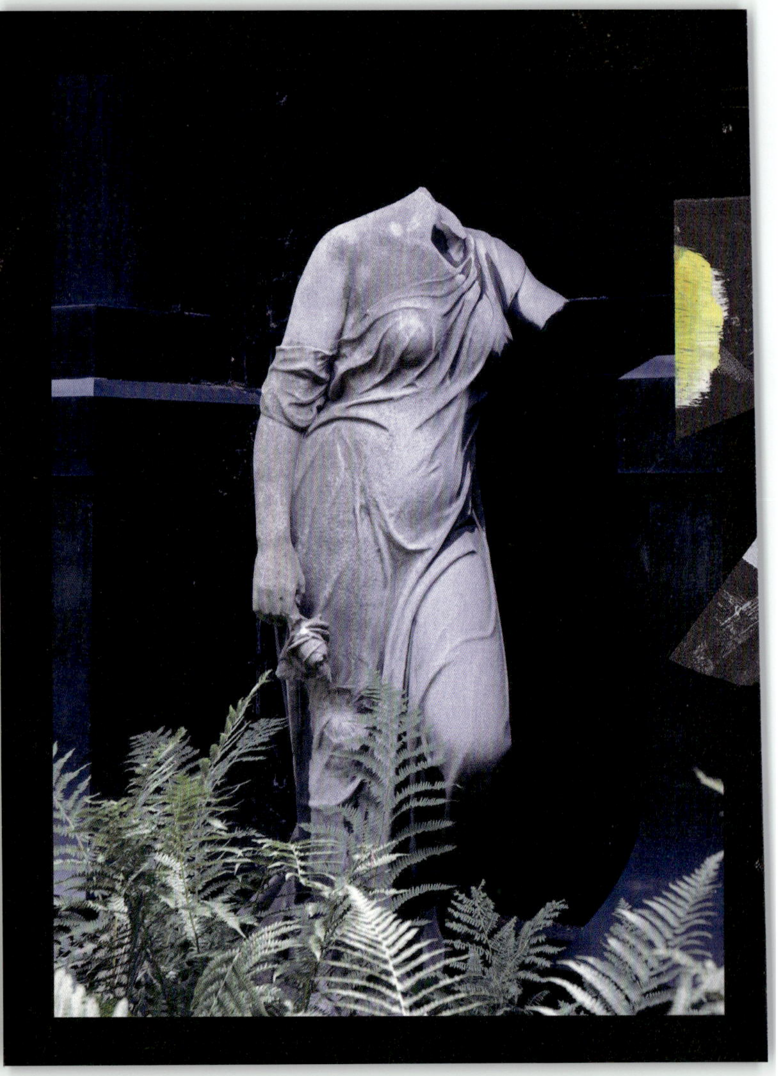

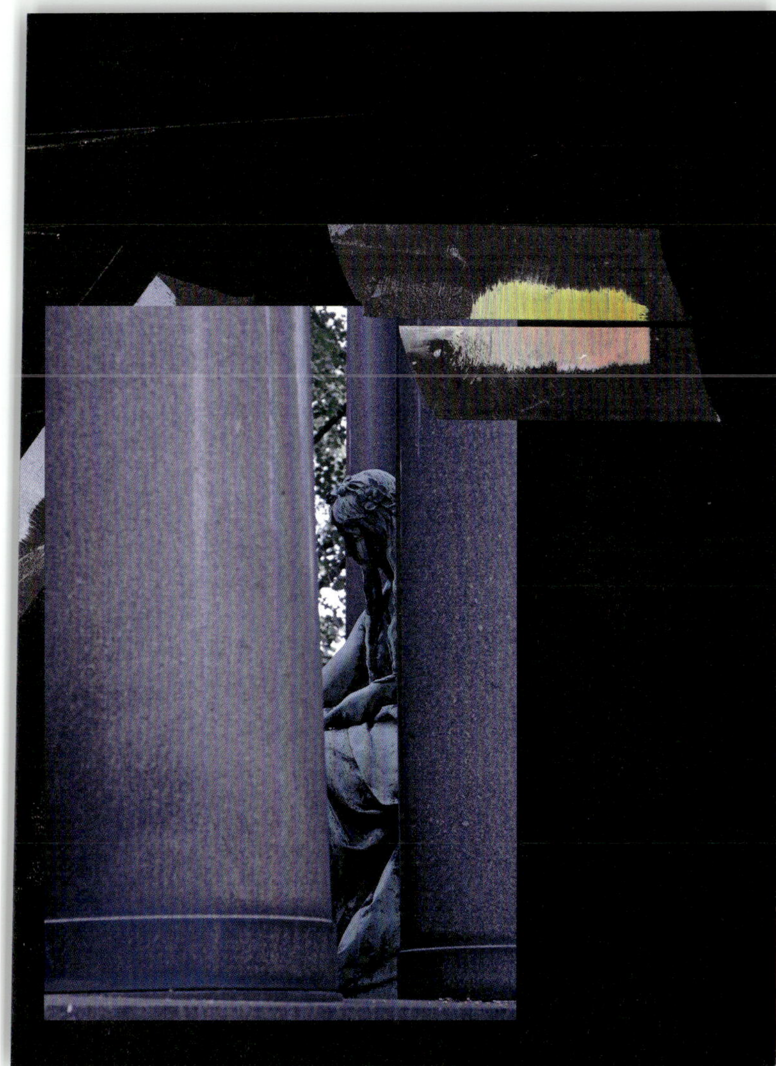

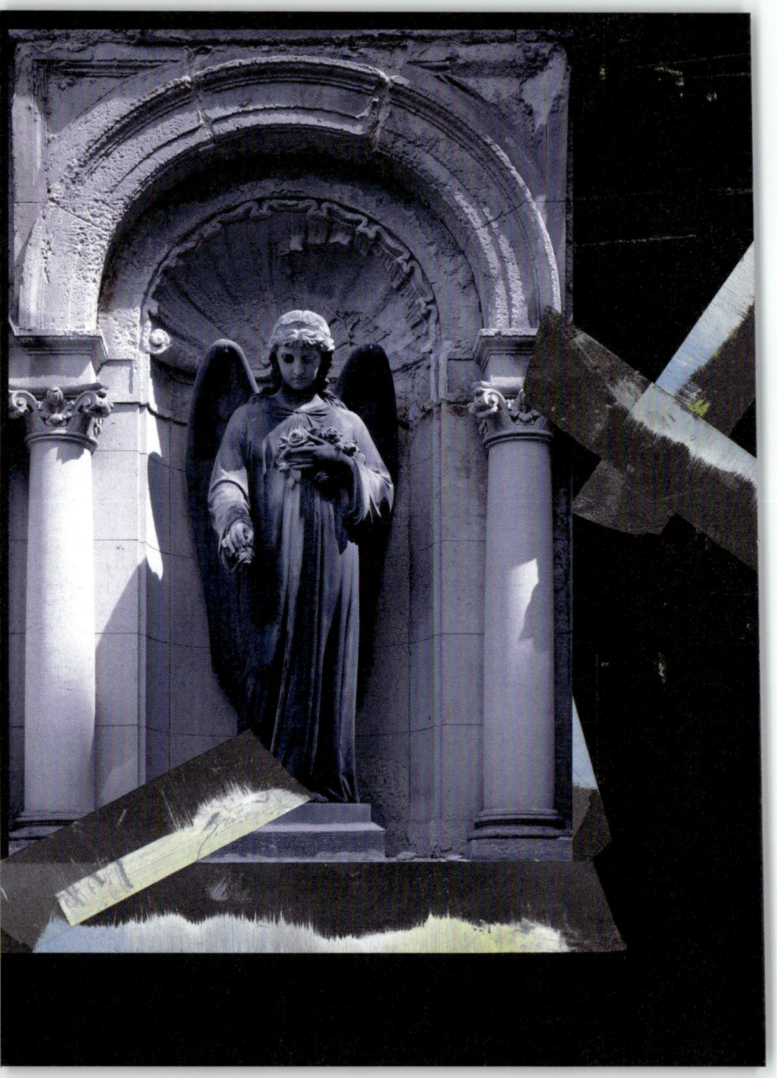

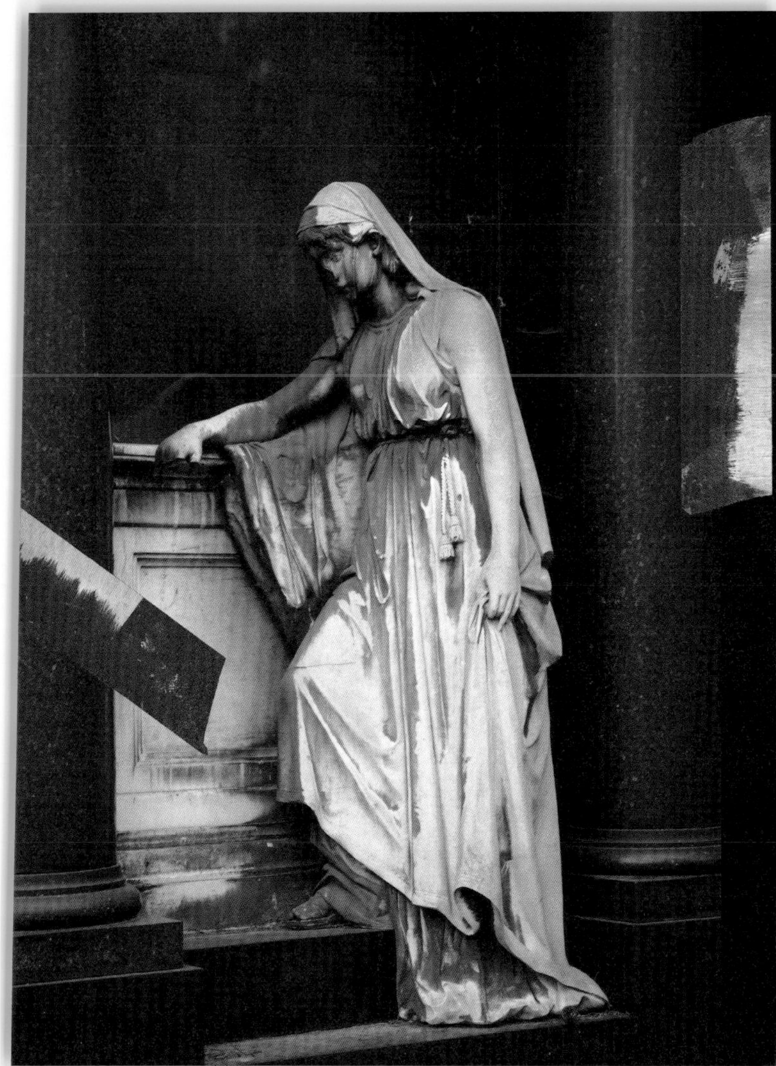

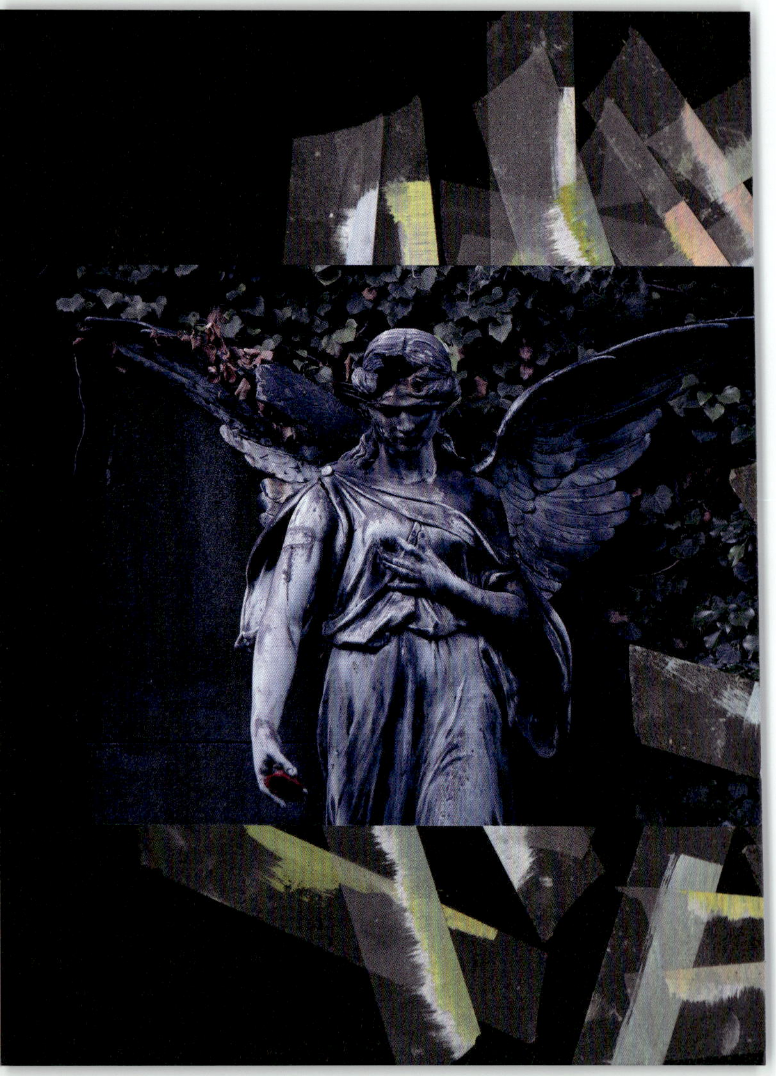

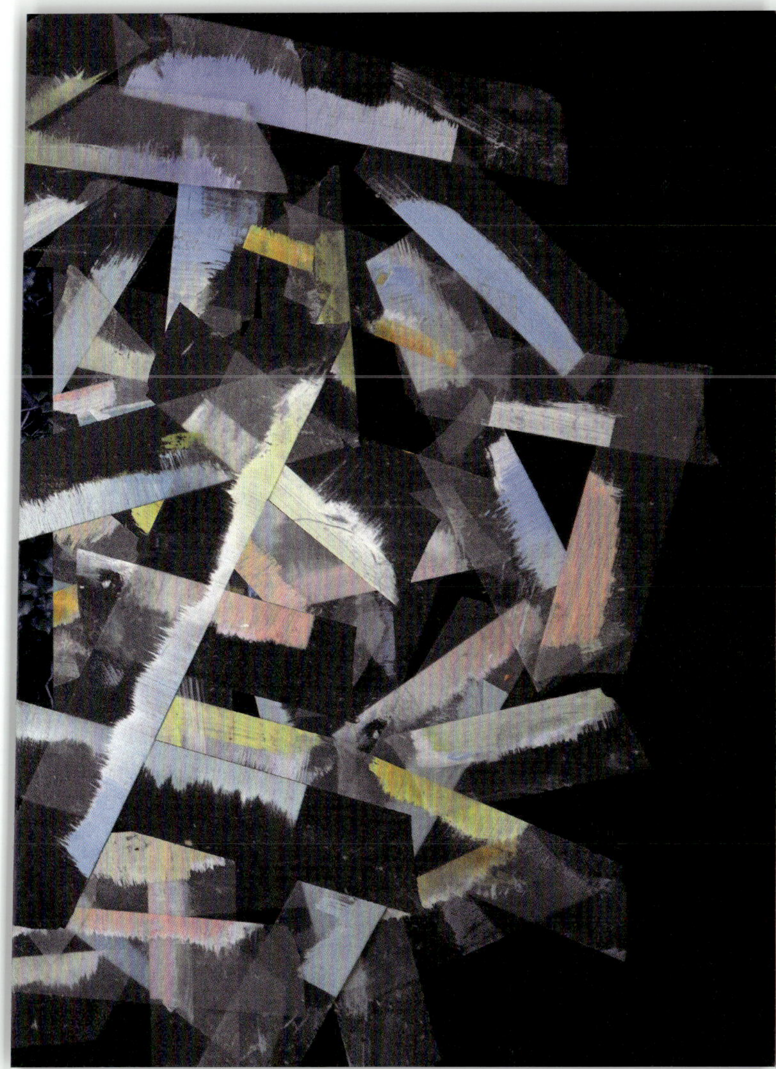

PHOTOGRAPHS

II. Sophienfriedhof, Berlin-Mitte, July 10, 2009

Jüdischer Friedhof, Berlin-Weissensee, July 12, 2009

Friedhof St. Andreas / St. Markus, Berlin-Weissensee, July 12, 2009

Friedhof IV der Jerusalems- und Neuen Kirche, Berlin-Kreuzberg, July 14, 2009

Friedrichswerderscher Friedhof II, Berlin-Kreuzberg, July 14, 2009

Dreifaltigkeitsfriedhof II, Berlin-Kreuzberg, July 14, 2009

Alter Luisenstädtischer Friedhof, Südstern, Berlin-Kreuzberg, July 14, 2009

Standortfriedhof, Lilienthalstrasse, Berlin-Neukölln, July 14, 2009

Garnisonsfriedhof, Columbiadamm, Berlin-Neukölln, July 14, 2009

Islamischer Friedhof, Columbiadamm, Berlin-Neukölln, July 14, 2009

Friedhof Heerstrasse, Berlin-Charlottenburg, July 19, 2009

Invaliden Friedhof, Berlin-Mitte, July 20, 2009

Friedhof der Oberpfau- und Domkirche zu Berlin, Berlin-Wedding, July 20, 2009

Französischer Friedhof, Berlin-Wedding, July 20, 2009

Friedhof der Domgemeinde St Hedwig, Berlin-Wedding, July 20, 2009

Friedhof II der Dorotheen Städtischen Gemeinde, Berlin-Wedding, July 20, 2009

Friedhof Adlershof, Berlin-Treptow, July 22, 2009

Friedhof der Evangelischen St. Laurentius Stadtkirchengemeinde, Berlin-Köpenick, July 22, 2009

Städtischer Friedhof in den Kisseln, Berlin-Spandau, July 25, 2009

Friedhof an der Gotlindestrasse, Berlin-Lichtenberg, August 1, 2009

Städtischer Zentralfriedhof Friedrichsfelde, Berlin-Lichtenberg, August 1, 2009

Parkfriedhof Marzahn, Berlin-Marzahn, August 1, 2009

II. Sophien Friedhof, Berlin-Mitte, August 3, 2009

I. St. Elisabeth-Friedhof, Berlin-Mitte, August 3, 2009

St. Thomas-Kirchhof, Berlin-Neukölln, August 9, 2009
Kirchhof Luisenstadt II, Berlin-Neukölln, August 9, 2009
St. Michael Kirchhof, Berlin-Neukölln, August 9, 2009
Kirchhof der Jerusalem und Neuen Kirche V, Berlin-Neukölln, August 9, 2009
St. Jacobi Kirchhof II, Berlin-Neukölln, August 9, 2009
Alter Sankt Matthäus Kirchhof, Berlin-Schöneberg, August 11, 2009
Zwölf Apostel Kirchhof, Berlin-Schöneberg, August 11, 2009
St. Luisen-Kirchhof III, Berlin-Charlottenburg, August 14, 2009
Friedhof der Evangelischen Kirchengemeinde Boxhagen-Stralau,
Berlin-Friedrichshain, August 17, 2009
Georgen-Parochial-Friedhof IV, Berlin-Friedrichshain, September 8, 2010

PAINTINGS

Oil on Tapes on Black Cutting Mat
Berlin, December 28, 2010 – January 6, 2011

TENDERNESS AND TEMPERATURE

Digital Image Processing
Berlin, January 7 – February 20, 2011

Caroline Bachmann and Stefan Banz have been involved in different joint projects since 2004. They work with photography, installation and painting, and live in Cully, Switzerland and Berlin, Germany. Website: www.bxb.ch

This book is dedicated to the living memory of Sophie, Burga, and Toinon.

We are deeply grateful to everybody who helped us realize this project, especially to Catherine Schelbert, John Brogden, Georg Rutishauser, Silvia Jaklitsch, Otmar Binder, David Sinclair-Jones, and Martina Buder.

KUNSTHALLE MARCEL DUCHAMP — N° 0

Editor
Kunsthalle Marcel Duchamp, Cully|Switzerland: www.bxb.ch/kunsthalle

Publisher
Verlag für moderne Kunst Nürnberg GmbH: www.vfmk.de

Concept, Artwork, and Layout
Stefan Banz and Caroline Bachmann

Lithography, Printing, and Bookbinding
DZA Druckerei zu Altenburg GmbH, Altenburg|Germany

ISBN
978-3-86984-241-7

Bibliographic information published by Die Deutsche Nationalbibliothek Die Deutsche Nationalbibliothek lists this publication in the Deutsche Nationalbibliografie; detailed bibliographic data is available on the Internet at http://dnb.ddb.de.